# Weaving the Literacy Web

Children's Books by Hope Vestergaard

*Hello, Snow!*

*Wake Up, Mama!*

*Driving Daddy*

*Baby Love*

# Weaving the Literacy Web

## Hope Vestergaard

Redleaf Press
St. Paul, Minnesota
www.redleafpress.org

Published by Redleaf Press
a division of Resources for Child Caring
10 Yorkton Court
St. Paul, MN 55117
Visit us online at www.redleafpress.org.

© 2005 by Hope Vestergaard

First edition published 2005
Cover and interior photos by Steve Wewerka
Interior design by Jill Wolf, Buuji, Inc.
Typesetting by Buuji, Inc.
The interior of this book was typeset in Cheltenham.

Redleaf Press books are available at a special discount when purchased in bulk for special premiums and sales promotions. For details, contact the sales manager at 800-423-8309.

Library of Congress Cataloging-in-Publication Data
Vestergaard, Hope.
    Weaving the literacy web : creating curriculum based on books children love / Hope Vestergaard.
      p. cm.
    ISBN-10: 1-929610-70-X (pbk.)
    ISBN-13: 978-1-929610-70-9 (pbk.)
    1. Reading (Early childhood)—Activity programs. 2. Children—Books and reading. 3. Early childhood education—Curricula. 4. Classroom libraries. I. Title.
    LB1139.5.R43V47 2005
    372.4—dc22

                                                                          2005005411

Manufactured in the United States of America
12   11   10   09   08   07   06   05      1   2   3   4   5   6   7   8

This book is printed on acid-free paper.

# Contents

# Acknowledgments

This book would still be a workshop if not for a nudge from Heidi McFadden, who said, "This could be a book, and I would buy it!" High praise from my former director, who did plenty of nudging and redirecting when I was a teacher in her care.

Thanks to Christine Kole MacLean—a friend, critic, and coach who coaxed me over the rough spots.

I'm also grateful for the support and encouragement of Gretchen Preston, who never doubted I could pull this off and who lets me use her classrooms as laboratories. Two people who inspired and informed my own development as a teacher are Laila Kujala Carmen and Margery Rushmer Heyl. Their habits of unleashing their own creativity in the classroom set a high standard for others to follow.

This book is infinitely richer for the contributions of many teachers, particularly LoisAnn Arnold and Megan VanderZee, who accepted all challenges with relish.

I couldn't have finished this book without all the faith, good cheer, snacks, and surprises that my family brought me in the batcave. *Tusind Tak!*

Last, many thanks to my editor, Beth Wallace, whose keen eye and sense of humor made this process *practically* painless.

Thank you, all!

# Introduction

When I was a child, books were the center of my world. They gave me adventures, information, and connections to the world and other people. As a curriculum consultant, I am always on the lookout for ways to help children experience books as I did. It eventually occurred to me: instead of planning curriculum around themes and finding books to match, why not begin with books? Starting with a book that children love helps teachers plan activities that are truly emergent because books reflect children's interests and needs. Book-based curriculum webs start with a great book and draw themes and activities from the story itself.

Planning activities that relate to books isn't a new idea, but building an entire curriculum around them is. This approach to planning has many benefits for children and staff. Reading to children early and often encourages a lifelong love of language and literature. Re-reading the same books increases phonemic awareness and allows children to practice important pre-reading skills such as recall, rehearsal, and prediction. Stories also provide a context for learning, helping children make connections across disciplines and build on existing knowledge. For teachers, book-based webbing helps ensure that curriculum responds to the children in their classes, and encourages collaboration with families. Planning is more efficient when ideas and activities can piggyback and build on each other, allowing more time for in-depth exploration of materials and processes. Last, but certainly not least, a classroom full of books conveys to children and families that literature is important.

# How I Came to Book-Based Webbing

There's no education like living and working with real, live kids. As a new teacher, I found that books cued many of my "aha" moments. When I read *The Little Mouse, the Red Ripe Strawberry, and the Big Hungry Bear* (Wood 1990) aloud, I noticed a twelve-month-old child sniffing the air for strawberries just before I turned to the sniffing page. When I recited the text for *Where the Wild Things Are* (Sendak 1964), wriggly toddlers would stay still long enough for me to help them into their snowsuits. And on the playground, I saw children of all ages acting out scenes or noticing elements of the stories they read. It was a thrill to see how early books become meaningful and captivating for young children. Reading and storytelling quickly became important tools in my teacher bag of tricks. Lesson planning, however, was still a challenge.

I hated filling in all the blanks on my center's form: gross motor, fine motor, sensory play, reading, etc., for every day of the week. It felt like a million slots to fill. We were never able to accomplish all the things we planned to do each day, so we decided to plan fewer, better activities. The director encouraged us to follow children's interests and plan open-ended activities. Our interest centers improved dramatically, even though we sometimes chose less-than-child-centered themes and used pre-planned units from resource books.

Fast-forward several years. After being a teacher for many years and a center director for several, I began consulting with early childhood programs in transition. I worked with a lot of teachers who were ready for a change. They wanted to plan activities that were more meaningful and engaging, but they didn't know where to start. I broke their tasks into smaller steps. I asked teachers to focus on one point of interest—an activity that most of the kids participated in and one that revealed something about their interests. I used the example of a favorite book as a concrete indicator of a child's interests and needs. Science, math, sensory play, etc., can all be found within the pages of a great story. Then I started thinking: rather than shoehorning books into themed units, why not *start* with the books? I invited teachers at several local child care centers to participate in a pilot program to build curriculum around books. Their experiences and responses led me to write this book.

# Shifting Gears

Think back to your first blank lesson plan as a new teacher. Were you intimidated or excited? Maybe a little of both. The endless possibilities are exciting—and overwhelming. Using a framework to plan lessons and activities makes the process more manageable. But if your lesson plans don't take into account the particular needs and interests of the children in your care, all your planning may be pointless. Experienced teachers may think that the way they currently plan works just fine. Why should either teacher bother with a new approach? Let's examine traditional methods and see how they stack up.

With *targeted planning,* lesson plans usually look like a grid, with columns for each day of the week and rows for several different interest areas. Many different kinds of programs use this kind of a form to plan curriculum. It's a useful tool because it includes spaces for activities in all areas of development and ensures a full schedule. But if teachers compartmentalize learning by plugging many different activities into the prescribed slots, children may not be encouraged or inspired to make connections among subjects. Making connections is the most basic way that children make sense of their world. Planning too many activities can also mean that exploration in each area is very basic, without opportunities to extend previous knowledge and form new understanding.

*Theme-based planning* is a more focused approach. Planning activities around a particular theme helps children make connections between the things they experience and the world around them. They can build upon knowledge in one area by applying the things they know to new situations. The problem with theme-based planning is that it can be difficult to choose an appropriate theme. Preselected themes may not be responsive to the children in the class. But leaving theme choices wide open can also be a problem because irrelevant or developmentally inappropriate themes focus curriculum in the wrong direction. There's also the temptation to develop theme-based units that are carved in stone. Even developmentally appropriate and engaging activity plans will grow stale if they don't evolve with the staff and children.

*Emergent curriculum* (Jones and Nimmo 1994) develops from children's needs and interests. It incorporates teacher, child, and parent interests and invites collaboration. Teachers consider children's needs as a group and on a day-to-day basis, enabling them to change gears when children are involved in or bored by activities. Truly emergent curriculum provides activities that allow children to explore their environment, manipulate materials, and discover information for themselves. The difficulty with emergent curriculum is knowing where to start. Adult filters affect the way we interpret the behaviors we observe; looking at the same classroom, several adults can have widely differing assessments. The challenge for teachers is to decide which behaviors truly represent the interests and needs that children may not be able to articulate for themselves.

*Book-based webbing* builds on the success of theme-based planning to make it more emergent. Books have built-in themes, and books children love reflect their interests and emotional needs. High-quality books have content to inspire activities in every interest area, allowing children to make connections and build on previous experiences.

In working with staff with a variety of backgrounds, I've found that even teachers who don't think of themselves as terribly creative can learn to plan book webs that are age-appropriate, relevant, and exciting. I personally have lots of ideas for using books in the classroom, but compiling them into a collection of completed webs doesn't make anyone else's curriculum more emergent. Instead, I decided to teach teachers how to weave their own webs. This book covers all the steps of webbing books—from planning to evaluation—so teachers can spin their own book-based curriculum webs.

## How to Use This Book

Chapter 1, "Weaving a Book-Based Web," contains the nitty-gritty, practical details of doing a book-based web, including sample timelines, preparation, material considerations, parent involvement, and wrapping up units to help children synthesize their observations and experiences.

Chapter 2, "Building Book-Based Activities," will help teachers jump-start their activity planning. For each interest area, it includes developmental considerations, questions to focus brainstorming sessions, and sample activities. There's also a troubleshooting guide.

Chapter 3, "Documentation and Evaluation," describes ways to preserve planning and activity materials for a variety of purposes: child development records, parent communication and education, teacher training, and future planning.

Chapter 4, "Introducing Book-Based Webbing to Staff and Families," outlines training and information sessions to help staff and parents learn about book-based webbing. I've included a few sample book webs for reference during training or for teachers to take for a test-drive.

Chapter 5, "Observing Children's Interests," will help teachers with a critical part of book-based webbing: selecting books that truly reflect children's needs and interests. It may be tempting to skip this legwork and select a book that you believe will work well, but for this process to be successful in the long term, you'll need to take time to reflect and respond to the individuals in your group.

Chapter 6, "Building a Classroom Library," discusses how to evaluate books for classroom use, how to find money for them in your budget, and how to store and display books to make them most useful. Even programs with strong, established libraries can benefit from doing the "Evaluating Books" exercise found at the end of the chapter.

Change can be scary. Depending on the experience and education you have, you (and your program) may be more or less prepared to shift your curriculum to be more book-based. Seasoned teachers already doing emergent curriculum may be ready to jump right into this new approach. Programs in transition may need to make the transformation in stages. If the entire process seems overwhelming, break it into manageable chunks. Adjust the pacing to allow staff time to really understand the process and become invested in it.

I'd like to close this introduction with a quotation from *Charlotte's Web* (White 1952):

> A spider's web is stronger than it looks. Although it is made of thin, delicate strands, the web is not easily broken. However, a web gets torn every day by the insects that kick around in it, and a spider must rebuild it when it gets full of holes.

Like a dusty web in the corner of a barn, a curriculum web in progress may look like a haphazard, tangled-up mess. But a closer look reveals that it's actually a thoughtfully woven network of interrelated ideas and concepts. Like Charlotte's webs in the book, the real marvel of curriculum happens when teachers and children take time to reflect and re-weave new layers of meaning and interest as they go.

# References

Jones, Elizabeth, and John Nimmo. 1994. *Emergent curriculum.* NAEYC 207. Washington, D.C.: National Association for the Education of Young Children.

Sendak, Maurice. 1964. *Where the wild things are.* New York: HarperTrophy.

White, E. B. 1952. *Charlotte's web.* New York: Harper.

Wood, Don and Audrey. 1990. *The little mouse, the red ripe strawberry, and the big hungry bear.* New York: Child's Play International.

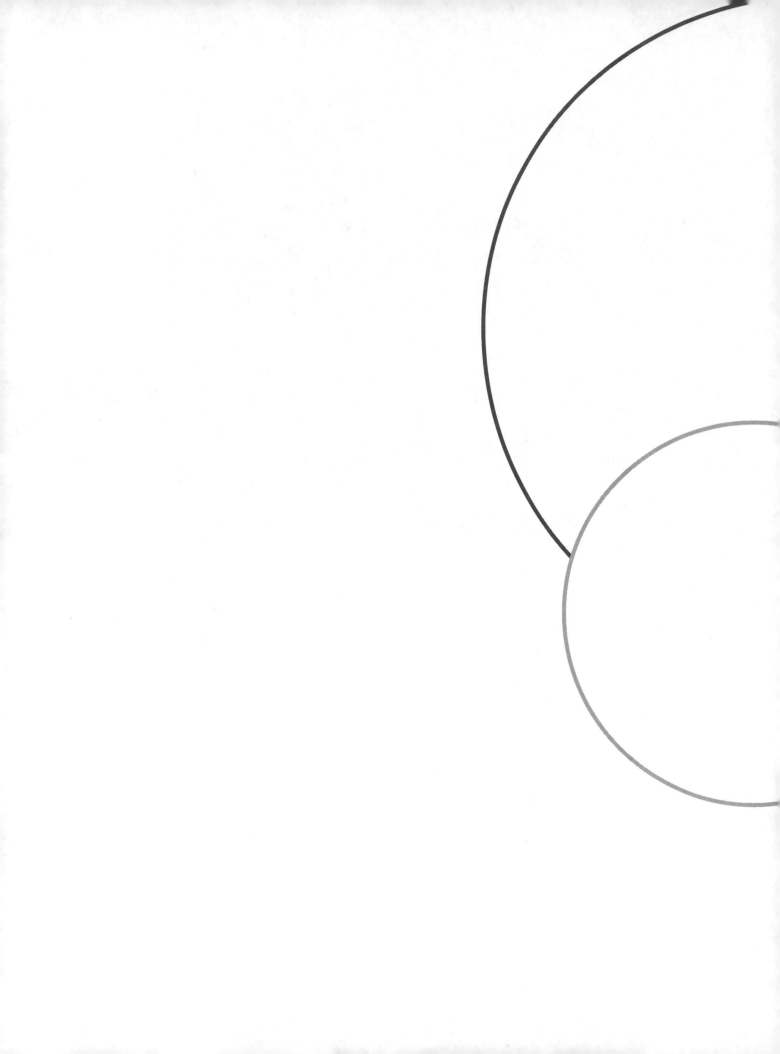

# 1 Weaving a Book-Based Web

"Emergent curriculum" describes an approach to planning in which ideas and activities are allowed to *emerge* as children participate. Instead of sticking to a preplanned activity that isn't working, teachers adapt plans based on the things that kids are responding to. If a class is doing a unit on space travel, teachers might start with an activity about packing a suitcase for a trip to outer space. Suitcase play could lead children to talk about other trips they have taken, which could lead a child to talk about a train trip, which could lead to train activities. Instead of trying to bring the focus back to space travel, teachers can follow the emerging interest. This philosophy values process over product.

A *curriculum web* is a tool for planning emergent curriculum. Teachers place a theme or concept at the center of a page, then spin off dozens of ideas (with input from the children if they're old enough). As the plan develops, teachers draw lines to connect related ideas in all directions, making a map that looks very much like a web. This format reminds teachers that good curriculum builds bridges between interest areas, rather than dividing them. *Book-based curriculum webs* are a way to ensure that curriculum is truly emergent because a good book may contain several interesting themes. Teachers can explore whatever elements of the story interest their group, rather than limiting curriculum to existing themes or plans.

On the facing page is a generic format for a book-based web. Later in this chapter and again in Chapter 4, you will see examples of completed webs in different formats.

A curriculum web can be a messy-looking prospect: activities and themes overlapping, new ideas spiraling in every direction. But just as with a spider's intricate web, there's a method to this madness. You start with the book and work outward. In this chapter, we'll walk step-by-step through a typical book unit and outline the time needed for all aspects of planning and doing a web.

# A Basic Book Web

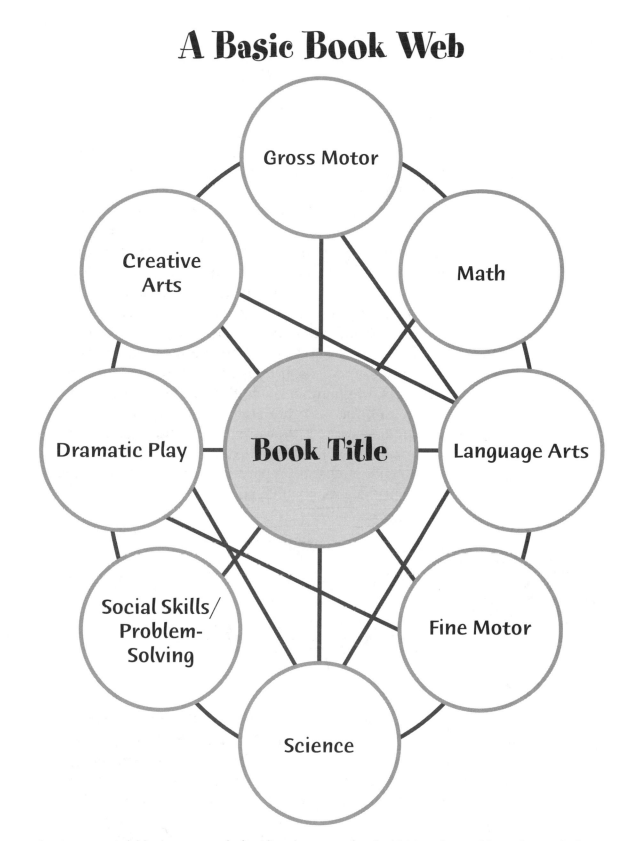

As you weave activities into your web, draw lines between related activities. The resulting web reveals the crossover among interest areas.

# Getting Started

Your early webs may be relatively short—one to two weeks long. As you grow more comfortable with book-based webbing, you will gain an instinctive sense of how long certain kinds of activities will sustain interest and become more efficient at planning a web full of satisfying experiences.

Being flexible with the end dates allows time to really respond to children's interests and build on experiences. In the beginning, however, you may have activities that fall flat, so don't be discouraged if a book web doesn't last as long as you expect it to. It's important to revisit successful and less successful activities to extend learning, to give children a chance to try new things, and to account for mood, staff energy, and other complicating factors. A web of activities for a good book typically lasts anywhere from two to four weeks. It depends on how concentrated your curriculum is, the number of children and staff involved, and your choice of book. As other staff and parents become comfortable with the new format, they are likely to suggest activities and related books that will help you extend your webs. If you allow a week for planning and preparation, expecting to complete one web per month is a reasonable goal.

# Your Web, Week by Week

The list on the following pages outlines the timing for a typical picture-book web. I've included these guidelines to help you accomplish all your goals, but they should not prevent teachers and children from taking an idea and running with it. Don't be too committed to specific dates. If an idea flops, reflect on it and move on. Our failures can tell us a lot about children's (and our own) needs and interests. Later, I'll outline all the steps in depth.

## Week One: Gearing Up

- Observe children for book favorites: 1–2 days.

- Discuss top choices for book, and pick a book to web: ½–1 hour.

- Brainstorm: 1–2 days. This includes circle time discussion with preschoolers and older children, staff discussion, and parent feedback.

- Gather materials: 1–2 days. This includes sorting existing materials, shopping for new supplies, and requesting donations from parents.

## Week Two: Diving In

- Day 1: Change bulletin boards and displays to reflect new book choice.

- Day 1: Send note home introducing book to parents.

- Day 1 and beyond: Stock and read related books.

- Days 2–4: Ask children: What do we know about _____? (Fill the blank space with one of the topics the children seem most interested in.) What do we want to know more about? Make lists of children's responses and use the "What we want to know more about" list to extend your activities.

- Day 5: Meet briefly with other staff to evaluate activities and plan for the following week.

- Days 1–5: Document as you go: notes, photos, and work samples.

## Week Three: Going Deeper (for high-interest webs)

- Continue to read related books and sing songs.

- Rotate or add to materials to enhance existing interest areas.

- Take a field trip or invite in a guest speaker/demonstrator.
- Document as you go.

## Week Four: Wrapping It Up

- Summarize the unit in a letter to parents and/or display.
- With the children, make a list of "what we learned" to be posted and incorporated into documentation. Post it where it can be compared with the "what we know" and "what we want to learn" lists from the beginning of the project.
- Take a field trip or invite in a guest speaker, or end with a party of sorts: prepare a special food or make a group piece of artwork to summarize the unit. Be sure to re-read the book!

Now that you have an overview of the process, let's look at each step in more detail.

# It's All in the Details: Planning and Preparation

When you choose a book to web, use one or more of the methods for observing children described in Chapter 5 to discover which books the children in your group find compelling. The more attention you pay at this point, the more appropriate your book choices will be. Be sure to observe two aspects of book behavior: children's responses to books when adults read them, and which books they seek out on their own. If you designate a spot on your parent bulletin board for book suggestions and encourage parents to post there, you can also incorporate home reading information into your planning.

If you team teach, make individual observations for possible books to web. Again, Chapter 5 has specific suggestions for observing children's interests. After observing children, designate a meeting time (at least half an hour) during which each teacher can pitch his or her suggestions and get feedback from other staff. This should be manageable in a napping classroom, or you can use a resource staff person to provide additional coverage in all the classrooms on a rotating basis. Set a time limit and number of recommendations per person to ensure that everyone has a chance to speak. Choose a book and share your decision with your supervisor, who may have valuable suggestions as you begin planning activities.

Brainstorming should be fun, fast, and furious. In a classroom notebook or on a clipboard in the staff lounge, record any and all ideas you have for activities relating to the book. Be sure to read other people's suggestions, as they may inspire you to look at the subject in a new way. In preschool and older classrooms, use circle time to introduce the web book and solicit children's ideas using open-ended questions such as these:

- What do you think this book will be about?
- Do you know any other books like this one?
- What do we know about [subject]?
- What do we want to know about [subject]?
- How can we learn more about [subject]?

Record children's suggestions on a dry erase board as you go. This shows children that words represent ideas, that ideas lead to other ideas, and that lists are a good way to help us organize our ideas. Here's an example of a a preschool group's brainstorming session with teacher notes for *My Little Sister Ate One Hare* (Grossman 1996):

## Children's Ideas

| | |
|---|---|
| what's a gizzard? | Play cards |
| what foods do you like? | there are patterns |
| what's a shrew? | what's a Polliwog? |
| why do people throw up? | peas taste good |
| wear costumes | there are shadows |
| do magic tricks | |

# Teachers' Notes

nutrition

group animals by traits

frog life cycle

food preference
    survey?

do math games with
    cards

pattern art

what is a pattern? find
    patterns

fantasy vs. reality

what's a homonym?

count what she ate

shrew vs. mouse, hare
    vs. rabbit--what's
    the difference?

weave baskets?

germs

 

Different parts of the process will take more or less time with various age groups. Teachers in infant classrooms will do all of the brainstorming, which is relatively quick. Gathering input from preschoolers takes more time, especially if they are adding many ideas. Older preschoolers, kindergartners, and early elementary children are likely to help speed up brainstorming because they will be familiar with the process and will be more accustomed to turn-taking, composing their thoughts, and expressing ideas.

After brainstorming, make a basic web plan on a large poster to be added to as you go. If you cannot make time for more in-depth planning together, divide duties so each teacher can add to it as he or she finds time. There are two ways to do this: have teachers plan by interest area, or have everybody contribute a certain number of activities to each interest area. There are advantages and disadvantages to both. When teachers plan by interest area, it can bring depth to the activities as individual interests and strengths come into play. Because some teachers are more adept than others in different areas, it will be important to rotate over time the interest areas you plan for. This way, teachers don't get in a rut and can model on others' successes to step outside of their own comfort zones. The posted web for *My Little Sister Ate One Hare* looked like this:

# A Book Web Example

**Gross Motor**
- Move like the animals in the book.
- Make a circus (balance, juggle, etc.).

**Creative Arts**
- Silhouettes
- Body outlines
- Color patterns.
- Make patterns.

**Math**
- Count and graph things she eats.
- Survey & graph food likes and dislikes.
- Play card games.

**Dramatic Play**
- Use flashlights to make hand shadows.
- Wear costumes like the characters.
- Split story and memorize to "read" aloud.

**My Little Sister Ate One Hare**
by Bill Grossman

**Language Arts**
- Sing "I Know an Old Lady Who Swallowed a Fly."
- Read cumulative stories.
- Write our own "Ate One..." story.
- Fantasy versus reality

**Social Skills/ Problem-Solving**
- Table manners when you try new foods
- What is an audience?

**Fine Motor**
- Simple magic tricks
- String games
- Cutting out pictures of animals from nature magazines

**Science**
- Sort animals by characteristics.
- What is a polliwog/ frog life cycle?
- Visit a nature center to see snakes, lizards, bats, etc.

When each teacher plans something for every interest area, it can bring breadth to activities by incorporating many different interests and skills. One challenge with this kind of planning is that the early bird gets the worm: the first person to record planning for any area can take the most obvious or what seem to be the most appealing activities, leaving the procrastinators or daydreamers to fill in the gaps. It can also limit the depth of activities because teachers may be less likely to capitalize on or develop others' ideas in favor of introducing their own.

The way you staff your classroom and run your interest centers also affects planning. I recommend that teachers each run the activities they have planned. In a classroom where one teacher works with assistants, you may need to delegate, but all staff should be encouraged to contribute ideas and management skills to the program.

Plan activities for each interest area, but remember that a single activity might involve several subjects: preparing fruit salad and eating it involves science (fruits and vegetables, growing, etc.), sensory discrimination (tasting and touching), math (counting, fractions), problem-solving skills (making a recipe), and self-help skills (cleanup). The goal is to provide just enough activities on a variety of topics so that the children in your room can find something that interests them and explore it in depth. Crossover content means fewer total activities and more time to do each; doing activities more than once allows children to build on their previous experiences and synthesize their discoveries.

## Shopping

On a weekly or monthly basis, you may need ingredients for cooking projects, craft supplies, or props for a dramatic play kit based on your book and themes. Many families have items at home that they are happy to donate. As soon as you begin spinning your web, present the book to parents. Send home a note to introduce the story and highlight the book itself in a special spot on the bulletin board, sign-in table, or display case. In your letter home, list some of the ideas you're working on and invite parents to contribute ideas. Here are some other items to include in the parent letter:

- a request for parents to share related books from home

- a general invitation for parents to participate in activities (list the specific ways they might participate with this unit)

- a specific invitation for parents to bring their special talents and interests to the unit: job-related skills, hobbies, cultural artifacts, and recipes are just a few examples

- words to songs or finger plays you'll be singing, so they can sing along with their children

- a specific request for any household items (specify whether it's a donation or a loan), such as dramatic play props, photos, etc.

Chapter 4 has an example of this kind of letter. At centers where parents volunteer regularly, teachers can post their planning web in a public area and invite parents to make notes on it.

## Diving In

Children's interests and questions should guide the webbing process as you go. As you begin a unit, use routine questions to spur discussion: *What do we know about _____? What do we want to know? Where can we find the answers?* As children dive into activities, use the following prompts to help you flesh out your web: *Do we have any other books about [this subject]? Can we find anything from this book at home? Does anybody's mom or dad know something about this?* With practice, children will begin asking these questions and making suggestions on their own. When kids pose theories, help them clarify them. Write their ideas on a sheet of paper and post it in the area of inquiry. Ask kids how they might test their ideas. Make a logbook to record results; have kids share these with parents or other staff. Once again, making this a traditional part of your exploration will inspire kids to do this without prompting.

As you do activities in the classroom, allow enough time for interested children to really get involved and double that amount to pique the interest of the ones who usually hang back. Do simpler activities earlier in the week. As children get excited about them, you can add materials or levels of challenge later in the week. If your activities go well—children are interested, engaged, and still using materials appropriately—you should consider a second week for your web. Select a few of the most popular activities and use these to guide your choices for new projects. Try to come up with projects that will tie together the various things the children have been exploring. For example, if you made a bulletin board or diorama relating to the book, you can add other elements or details, such as plants or animals to an outdoor scene or details from the book to an indoor scene. If the kids created something useful, you can find homes for these objects in the community: a local business; an art show; a local park (get permission from your local government first). Extending your activities outside the center helps kids connect what they are doing at the center with the real world and helps them feel like powerful members of the community. Chapter 2 has specific ideas and suggestions for planning and working with open-ended activities.

# Wrapping It Up

As a web winds down, it's important to reflect on successes and areas for improvement. Class meetings provide closure and allow children to review and delight in all they have learned. As a group, compile a list called "What we learned from [insert book title]" to post. Let children see you copy these lists into a class notebook, and refer to them later whenever they have questions. This teaches kids that their observations are important, that they can build on knowledge, and that they can share what they know with others in a meaningful way. Taking note of questions children still have will help guide future web planning. (Chapter 3 has more specific suggestions on ways to evaluate children's web experiences.) For less verbal children, art is a great way to document their impressions. Ask them to draw pictures about the book. Don't tell children what the picture should be; just see what they come up with. Display these on a bulletin board together and include informative notes about individual interests and/or child development. (Chapter 4 has several suggestions for using work to explain children's development to parents).

Newsletters and regular letters home are great ways to bridge the home-school information gap. Sharing informative and entertaining kid quotes about web activities for your newsletter gives parents a starting point for conversations about school. Choose quotes that represent the range of experience, such as the examples in the *Dinosaurs* lists and web starting on p. 81. Parents also benefit from reading a detailed summary of the webs you do. These summaries keep them informed about the great things going on in the classroom and give them ideas for activities to continue play at home. After each unit, take time to compile a brief list of your activities and learning outcomes for each. (Chapter 5 discusses many additional ways to share information about curriculum with parents and the community.) Here's the summary (or compiled web) for *My Little Sister Ate One Hare*.

## Creative Arts

- Draw silhouettes of children using a utility lamp (artistic method, imitation).

- Trace body outlines and decorate (gross and fine motor work, synthesis).

- Create patterns using construction paper and bingo markers (math, problem-solving).

## Math

- Count the total number of things she eats (one-to-one correspondence).

- Graph the things she eats (representation).

- Ask children if they like to eat peas (yes or no). Graph the result (representation, information gathering).

- Ask parents if they like peas and add to the graph (synthesis).

- Play card games: war (greater than/less than, counting), crazy eights (matching), go fish (matching, set recognition, counting).

## Fine Motor

- Practice magic tricks: disappearing cup, sugar cube trick (coordination, confidence).

- Do string games like cat's cradle, Jacob's ladder, etc. (hand-eye coordination, problem-solving, repetition).

## Gross Motor

- Move like the animals (coordination, imitation).

- Make a circus act: balance beam, juggling, stacking plastic cups (hand-eye coordination, balance).

## Language Arts

- Read *Joseph Had a Little Overcoat* (Taback 1999), *My Little Sister Hugged an Ape* (Grossman 2004), and *The Dress I'll Wear to the Party* (Neitzel 1992).

- Sing "I Know an Old Lady Who Swallowed a Fly."

- Talk about *homonyms*: hare/hair, hear/here, we/wee, too/two, red/read, etc. Make spelling cards with pictures for the word box (phonemic awareness, spelling patterns, handwriting).

# Science

- Sort animals by characteristics: legs/no legs; hairy/not hairy; big/little; scary/not scary, etc. (traits, comparison, classification).

- Catch polliwogs and watch them grow into frogs (life cycle).

- Visit the nature center to see real snakes, bats, lizards, and mice.

- Discuss the difference between a hare and a rabbit; a mouse and a shrew; a frog and a toad (vocabulary, classification).

# Social Skills/Problem-Solving

- Talk about table manners—what to do when you don't like or know the food. Talk about polite words and no-thank-you bites (problem-solving, empathy).

- What is an audience? Practice being an audience with good behavior: be quiet and still, clap, pay compliments, or ask questions (listening skills).

# Dramatic Play

- Use flashlights to make hand shadows (cooperation, imitation).

- Dress up like the little sister's characters (expression, role playing).

- Use regular costumes and ask, What would this character like to eat? (prediction, role-playing)

- Pick yucky foods (grass, worms, etc.) and guess who would eat them (prediction, turn-taking).

As you can see from this web's development, some items on the brainstorming list didn't end up being used, and others were added. This is typical: when you allow children to become engrossed in some activities, you may not have time or interest for other things you've planned.

# Looking Ahead

A book-based curriculum web is a wonderful way to promote positive attitudes about reading and ensure that curriculum responds to children's interests. Saving materials from successful webs will help teachers explain the process with parents and new staff. Even book webs that flop are good teaching tools. But there's no reason for your web to flop! Now that you have an overview of the webbing process, Chapter 2 will help you plan activities that are relevant, developmentally appropriate, and engaging.

# References

Grossman, Bill. 1996. *My little sister ate one hare.* New York: Crown.

Grossman, Bill. 2004. *My little sister hugged an ape.* New York: Knopf.

Jones, Elizabeth, and John Nimmo. 1994. *Emergent curriculum.* NAEYC 207. Washington, D.C.: National Association for the Education of Young Children.

Neitzel, Shirley. 1992. *The dress Ib,./ll wear to the party.* New York: Greenwillow.

Taback, Simms. 1999. *Joseph had a little overcoat.* New York: Viking.

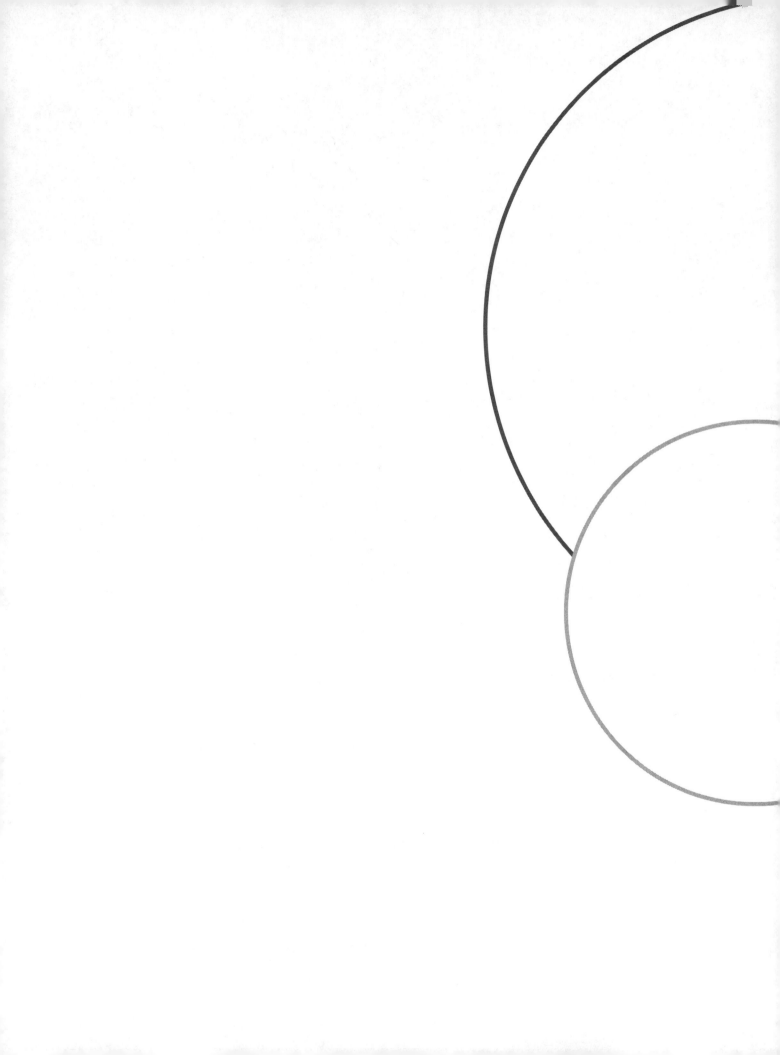

# 2 Building Book-Based Activities

Open-ended, developmentally appropriate activities are the backbone of a book-based curriculum web. For experienced teachers, this chapter outlines ways to transform closed-ended activities to make them more child-centered and emergent. For teachers in search of new curriculum ideas, this chapter poses questions to inspire brainstorming and suggests starter activities for each interest area. Both new and experienced teachers can use the "Ages and Stages" guidelines for each interest area to ensure that activities are developmentally appropriate. Finally, we'll discuss common implementation problems and ways to address them.

# Open-Ended Teaching and Learning

Have you ever been interested in improving a particular skill—say, for example, drawing and painting? Which of the following classes would you rather take?

> Class A: Mastering the Masters! Your teacher, Suzy Sizemore, will show you what's great about great art. She'll teach students to create pictures in the style of her own award-winning collage, *All the Places I've Been.* At the end of the session, we'll have a juried art show with prizes for the best work.

> Class B: Take Apart Art! Participants will "disassemble" masterpieces to examine individual elements of great art. We'll explore various media firsthand and create work in students' chosen media. At the end of the session we'll collaborate on a group project to be displayed at the library.

Both classes will expose students to great art, which can be inspiring and educational. But Class A's instructor has a very narrow definition of success for her students. If your skills and artistic taste don't meet her standards, the class might be discouraging. Class B's instructor has no particular product in mind other than a group effort at the end of the class. She plans to share tools and techniques that students can apply to their own interests. Students in both classes will learn new art techniques. But Class A's students will win or lose, depending on how closely they can meet one set of criteria; Class B's students will work toward personally satisfying projects and increased comfort with the process. Adult learners are no different from child learners: we want consideration of our abilities; we want a chance to be creative; we want to figure things out for ourselves. This is why planning open-ended activities makes teaching more satisfying and enriching for students and facilitators.

Experienced teachers with little or no exposure to emergent curriculum may be able to reshape existing activity plans to make them more open-ended. The example below illustrates the limitations of narrow focus activities and how they can be made more appropriate.

# Example: Do artwork inspired by the book.

Closed-end activity: "Copy this page or specific technique." Successful outcome: Picture is recognizable from the book.

Open-ended activity: "Draw something from the book" (don't specify what). "Make something using art techniques/media from the book."

Successful outcomes:

- Comprehension: art incorporates book elements

- Fine motor practice: child experiments with artistic techniques from the book

- Art appreciation: child composes a picture

- Visual discrimination: child notices artist's technique

- Problem-solving: child figures out a way to make his art look like the artist's

# Planning for Interest Centers

Planning activities that involve more than one interest area helps kids make connections across the curriculum and makes each activity appealing to different children. It's also a more efficient way of teaching, since trying to accomplish several different activities in a block of time is difficult. So much time goes to setting up materials and cleaning up, it leaves little time for children to become engrossed. Activities on any given day should target all the interest areas, but if you plan just a few activities that overlap, you will give children more time to explore each one and extend learning. For ease of planning, I've divided activities into eight content areas:

- Creative Arts

- Dramatic Play

- Fine Motor Activities

- Gross Motor or Movement Activities

- Language Arts

- Math

- Science

- Social Skills and Problem-Solving

I've outlined three elements of planning for each interest area: *developmental issues, questions to consider* as you read the book, and *sample activities*. Activities are grouped by age level, but older kids can do any of the younger activities that appeal to them. Keep in mind that these sample activities are merely starting points.

# Creative Arts

Creative arts include art exploration and music. Art exploration activities should emphasize process over product. Music activities should involve listening skills, rhythmic play, and producing musical sounds with real and homemade instruments. The classroom emotional environment should be supportive and accepting to encourage children to be expressive and take risks.

## Ages and Stages

*Infants and toddlers* benefit greatly from exposure to music. Music and movement are important for children's emotional well-being and physical development. Babies can be sensitive to environmental factors, so be sure that music choices (when to play it, what to play, how loud, etc.) take into consideration the children's immediate needs. Expressive art tends to focus on exploration of materials—scribbling and playing with color, glue, etc.—as children are still developing fine motor control and learning how to use lines and shapes to represent real objects.

*Preschoolers* love to create and listen to all kinds of music; they will physically respond to music by quickening their pace, etc., so teachers can use music to set the tone for classroom activities. Artwork often includes recognizable subject matter, but children still spend a fair amount of time experimenting with different media. As children learn to use shapes and lines to illustrate objects, they may copy other drawings or model on real objects.

# Questions for Teachers

## Creative Arts

- What are the colors, textures, and shapes in this story?

- What medium did the illustrator use? Can my students produce elements of this kind of art? Can it be simplified?

- What elements of the story (for example, leaves, things with wheels) can we use as artistic tools?

## Music

- What are the natural sounds in this story?

- Does this story use any familiar melodies or songs that we can learn?

- How can my students re-create the sounds of this story?

# Sample Creative Arts Activities

## For All Ages

- Provide art materials from the book for exploration. Choose *color* or *texture* or *technique* (for example, Eric Carle's torn, painted paper), and let the children explore.
  The following questions will guide art exploration of color and texture: *What are the colors in this book? How do we mix these colors with paint? Where do we find these colors in nature? How do these colors make us feel?* Explain the word *texture,* the way something feels: smooth or bumpy, soft or hard, etc. Then ask these questions: *How do you think this object feels? What else feels like that? How can we make something feel like that? Where do we find this texture in nature? Why is this texture in this book?*
  *Technique* involves the tools and materials the artist used. Some simple questions to jumpstart a technique discussion: *How do you think the artist made this picture?*

*Is this art drawn or painted or shaped?* With experience, you can be more specific: *How did the artist draw these lines? Did they use pen or pencil or something else?* With collage or clay or other dimensional art, ask children if any part of the picture looks like anything they have ever seen. Experiment with some materials (playdough versus clay, for example) to figure out which one is closest to the effect in the book. Explore the medium used in the book simply at first: provide paper, paint, and standard brushes, for example. Then encourage kids to find other tools that can enhance or change the appearance. With art that uses several steps (for example, Eric Carle's painted and torn paper), have the children guess how they might create the same effect.

- Explore a particular medium using various techniques. For example, with paint, you might try brushes, stamps, fingers, tools, cars, etc.

- Build a bulletin board based on the book. Have the children determine what to include, and post the items on it over time.

- Put drawing paper in interesting areas of the room: under a table, on the wall, on the floor, etc.

## For Infants

- In a high chair, let children explore colors from the book using nontoxic paint (cornstarch and water with a drop or two of food coloring).

- In an empty plastic swimming pool, let babies play with nontoxic "paint" and paper.

## For Toddlers and Up

- Use paint to mix the colors for the story.

- Move art play outside so children can be inspired by the outdoors.

- Explore art in your community. Visit museums or outdoor sculpture; pay attention to landscaping, architecture, etc., as they pertain to your book.

## For Preschoolers and Up

- Trace around objects from the book.

- Cut pictures out of magazines that depict objects from the book.

- Have children draw silhouettes of each other and decorate them as characters from the book.

- Make paper bag or sock puppets from the book.

## For Older Preschoolers and Kindergartners

- During a field trip, have children pick a piece of art they'd like to emulate back at the center. (Photograph sculpture or three-dimensional art for reference, or make a list together of the things you'll need.)

- Invite a local artist to do a demonstration at the center.

- Stage an art exhibit at a local business. Include brief written explanations for onlookers.

# Sample Music Activities

## For All Ages

- Sing songs that relate to the story.

- Use (or make and use) rhythm instruments and streamers to move with music.

- Write new words to familiar tunes that incorporate elements of the book.

- Play background music in the dramatic play, science, and fine motor interest areas.

- Find natural sounds that occur in the story. Try to recreate them using classroom objects; listen to the real sound (using audio files from the Internet or nature CDs and tape recordings).

# Dramatic Play

Dramatic play includes formal and casual role-playing such as performing with puppets or as actors. Children's dramatic play often mirrors real-life issues. Teachers provide a "safe" setting where children can practice dealing with real-life challenges. Teachers should be available to coach children and offer suggestions, with less direction as children get older.

## Ages and Stages

*Infants and toddlers* begin to play symbolically (for example, use a block for a telephone) at about one year of age. Very young children love to play with toys that look like "off-limits" grown-up items: telephones, keys, cash registers, etc. As they begin representational play, toddlers and young preschoolers grow increasingly inventive and use everyday items to act out their stories and reenact events in their lives.

*Preschoolers* love role-playing. Many younger children will still need guidance to share props and negotiate turns; older children are able to memorize short plays and act them out. Any performance art should be freewill. Often students will first observe from the sidelines before they jump in.

## Questions for Teachers

- What props could we use to role-play scenes from this story?

- What existing dramatic play prop boxes relate to this story?

- What developmental challenges in this book could my children explore using dramatic play? (for example, sharing, loss, anger management, etc.)

# Sample Dramatic Play Activities

## For Infants and Young Toddlers

- Provide safe props from the book (for example, muffin tins, spoons) for children to play with.

- Do finger plays relating to your web.

- Use felt board pieces to retell the story individually or during group time.

- Use puppets to act out parts of the story.

## For Toddlers and Up

- Incorporate props from the stories into your dollhouse.

- Make paper bag puppets.

## For Preschoolers and Up

- Build age-appropriate dramatic play kits based on elements of the story.

- Put on a play based on the story using simple props for costumes.

- Take turns retelling the story at circle time.

## For Older Preschoolers and Kindergartners

- Videotape your performance. Assign jobs: director, actors, stagehands, etc.

- Make sock puppets to go with the book.

# Fine Motor Activities

Fine motor play includes puzzles, sensory play, and manipulatives such as blocks, pegs, and Lego building blocks, as well as some creative arts activities. Fine motor play also provides many opportunities for problem-solving.

## Ages and Stages

*Infants and young toddlers* develop fine motor control at widely varying rates. Repetitive small muscle activity can be fatiguing and frustrating, so follow children's individual cues. Sensory play with children who are still very oral should involve nontoxic materials (cornstarch and water, homemade playdough, and so on) or large items—swatches of fabric, large manipulatives, or whole-body sensory play. Sand should be free of small stones; any small objects used in bulk should be evaluated for choking hazards.

*Preschoolers* have increasing fine motor control and enjoy tasks that involve this kind of skill—cutting, building, and fitting things together. Some young preschoolers still explore objects orally, so supervision with sensory materials is advisable. If children are frustrated by intricate tasks, consider ways to increase the scale of the work you're doing. Fine motor control is a key pre-reading skill, but don't expect children under age six to be able to print letters neatly. The acts of cutting, painting, and piecing things together exercise the muscles needed for printing in elementary school.

## Questions for Teachers

- Are there handcrafts in this story?
- Are there things that fit together in this story? Are there things that can be taken apart?
- Does this book have small objects that can be collected and manipulated?

# Sample Activities with Manipulatives

## For Infants and Toddlers

- Provide collections of toys from the book (trains, animals, etc.) for children to sort and line up, drive on a tape line, or place in and take out of small containers.

- Glue pictures from copies of book pages onto frozen juice concentrate lids for children to match, sort, and stuff into a container.

## For Preschoolers and Up

- Build small-scale structures from the book using age-appropriate classroom manipulatives.

- Build objects from the book using recycled materials.

- Play with playdough using book props, colors, and scents.

## For Older Preschoolers and Kindergartners

- Sew, iron on, or color quilt squares for a book blanket.

- Make shoebox dioramas or Popsicle stick puppets for story scenes.

# Sample Sensory Play Activities

## For All Ages

- Fill the sensory table with age-appropriate wet, dry, solid, and liquid materials and tools that relate to the story or story setting.

- Make recipes from the books.

- Taste, smell, and touch sensations from the story.

- Play with playdough (older toddlers and up) that is scented and/or colored like something from the book; use interesting tools from the book with the playdough.

# Gross Motor or Movement Activities

Gross motor play, indoors and out, improves children's strength, flexibility, and coordination. It's also a great outlet for their boundless energy!

## Ages and Stages

*Infants* develop at widely varying rates. Very young babies develop muscle control from being in many different positions: lying down, being held, etc. Propped on their tummies with a towel roll under their arms, they can use their hands to explore objects. Infants who sit up can use their hands for gross motor play; held in a teacher's lap or arms (for a short period of time), they can bounce, kick, and explore materials with their feet. Crawling infants and young toddlers love to explore all kinds of spaces with their whole bodies. Most babies love to dance; the appropriate tempo and range of movement will vary from child to child.

*Toddlers* love to fill and dump containers and manipulate large objects (boxes, balls, push toys, child furniture) in their environment. Things with wheels are particularly interesting, and moving large push toys and vehicles involves a lot of muscle work. Toddlers also love to throw things; encourage them to throw beanbags and soft balls instead of other toys, and give them bins or something to aim at. Music helps toddlers focus on particular kinds of gross motor work. Remember never to put children of any age into a position they could not get into on their own—for example, the top of the climber. If they can't safely climb up to it, they can't safely get down.

*Preschoolers* have increasing muscle control and enjoy specific physical challenges such as throwing something at a target, balancing, or playing ball with a friend. Older preschoolers have more stamina than young children and will benefit from activities that involve deep muscle work: walks, moving heavy objects around the playground, climbing, digging, swinging. Children who are fidgety and distractible in class may need focused gross motor play to help them channel excess energy.

# Questions for Teachers

- What kinds of movement are in this story? Think about characters: if they're people, do they move in interesting ways? If they're animals, how do they move?

- What do the characters use their muscles for?

# Sample Gross Motor Activities

## For Infants

- Help them move like characters in the story: take a wagon ride, pull them in a sled or on a towel, swing them in your arms, etc.

- Give them large cardboard boxes to explore with their whole bodies.

- Glue or use contact paper to attach photocopied pictures from the book to gross motor props: large cardboard tubes, small boxes, undersides of climbers, etc.

- Hang soft objects from the book on an activity gym for them to bat with their hands or kick at.

- Dance with them on your lap or in your arms.

## For Toddlers and Up

- Do the muscle work involved in the story. Is there building? Gardening? Dancing?

- Move like the characters. If there are animals in the book, start out moving like them; then challenge the children to move like other animals that are similar and different.

- Use masking tape to mark a "balance beam" path on the floor.

- Build a house or spaceship or a structure from the book using large cardboard boxes and duct tape. Decorate it together!

- Fill a plastic swimming pool with sensory materials for a whole-body experience.

## For Preschoolers and Up

- Make a developmentally appropriate obstacle course indoors or out that incorporates elements of the story.

- Use twigs or milk crates or other moveable objects outdoors to make a "map" of something from the book: a neighborhood, a home, a journey.

- Make a target or use a basket to toss things from the book into: balls, bean bags, acorns, etc.

## For Older Preschoolers and Kindergartners

- Have children do two-person exercises such as boat-rowing or other movements from the book.

- Have children design an obstacle course and time themselves going through the course.

- Teach children line, square, or folk dances.

- Have children make up their own stomps or chants that relate to the book.

# Language Arts

"Literacy" encompasses pre-reading behaviors, actually learning to read, and most important, developing an appreciation of and affection for reading. Language arts skills include listening, articulation, and comprehension of spoken language.

# Ages and Stages

*Infants* like to explore books with their hands and mouths. They enjoy listening to rhythmic chants and imitating finger plays. They love books that use sound words and simple, lyrical language. Fabric books and sturdy board books are good for this age group; adults can model appropriate book handling behaviors such as gentle touches and page turns. Babies are kinetic listeners, so they may move around as they listen. Holding an object related to the story can help them sit longer to listen.

*Toddlers* love rhyming and predictable stories that let them anticipate their favorite parts. Most toddlers can handle board books appropriately with guidance. They may not have the fine motor control (or impulse control) to handle the thin pages of regular books. Toddlers are still kinetic listeners and may get up and move around during story time. Props help reduce fidgeting. Children's receptive vocabularies, or the words they understand, are much larger than their expressive vocabularies, the words they can produce.

*Preschoolers* become more focused on their peers than on adults, so they show increased interest in books about relationships outside the family. Most preschoolers can handle books appropriately with occasional reminders. Although they may listen on the run as they play and work, they can also sit and listen to a lively story at circle time. Quiet, reflective books are best with small groups of children and should be accompanied by cues such as lowered lights to help them settle down.

Some *four-year-olds* show an interest in letters and words and may even match words to pictures. Most understand that particular words belong on each page of a story. They can recite passages by heart and will correct adults who skip or change words. *Four-*, *five-*, and *six-year-olds* begin to draw narrative pictures rather than single scenes and may ask to dictate their words to a teacher who will write them down. Teachers should encourage beginning readers to express their ideas rather than focusing on the specific mechanics of spelling and phonics.

# Questions for Teachers:

- Describe the story in a single sentence. This summary will help you think about the big picture.

- What is the structure of this story? (See Chapter 6 for descriptions of kinds of stories.)

- Can I find activities that mirror this story's structure?

- What do the children love about this book?

# Sample Language Arts Activities

## For All Ages

- Make a felt board version of the book. (Use simple lines and main characters/elements, or find templates online and in teacher books.)

- Have teachers tell the story to the group using the felt board.

- Leave the felt board open for children to tell stories to each other during free choice time.

- Record teachers or parents reading classroom books. Include sounds to signal page turns for older children.

- Sing songs and do finger plays that relate to elements of the story at circle time, with meals, and during transitions. Post the words to songs and finger plays, and send copies home so parents can learn them.

- Make story bags that include a copy of a book, props, and a simple game or activity related to the story. Take turns sending the bags home with students for an evening to read with their parents.

- Do an Internet search on your book's title and author. Many publishers, authors, and illustrators have printable materials and activity suggestions relating to their books.

## For Toddlers and Up

- Have children dictate the story in their own words.

- Ask a question about the story (for example, "What is a secret?"), and post the children's responses.

- Make a simple picture recipe relating to the book.

- Find poems related to your book. Read them. Memorize them. Have children perform them.

- With books that employ alliteration, have fun with the letters involved in various activities. Brainstorm and play with words that share the same sounds.

## For Preschoolers and Up

- Have children illustrate the story on a storyboard. If the children can't write but want to include text, have them dictate captions to their images.

- Use words and pictures to make a recipe. After the cooking project, have children dictate the steps and any conclusions or comments.

- Have children take turns telling the story (using a book or felt board pieces) in their own words as other children listen.

- Use guides for "Show and Tell" objects: "Bring something that begins with [high frequency letter from the book]" or "Bring something from home that you can see in this book," etc.

- Have children go on a letter hunt in the classroom, using clipboards to draw pictures of items (or spell them phonetically if they can) that begin with the same sound.

## For Older Preschoolers and Kindergartners

- Have children make their own felt board pieces.

- Discuss whether the story is realistic or fantasy.

- Make copies of book pages and cut out pictures of the main characters and story elements. Print keywords on index cards, and glue the photocopied pictures on the back. Let children manipulate these at the writing center. They may play a guessing game with them, they might practice spelling, or they might try to match magnetic letters to the letters in each word to see how the sounds combine to form words.

- With older children, use comprehension prompts: Who is this book about? What does he or she want? How does he or she get it?

# Math

Children begin to understand math concepts such as addition and subtraction long before they have the vocabulary to describe these things. Early childhood classrooms should provide a variety of concrete materials for children to sort, count, and group. This allows individuals to experiment and explore at their own pace.

## Ages and Stages

*Infants' and toddlers'* pre-math behaviors include collecting, dumping, filling, sorting, and working with simple puzzles. Toddlers learn to count without understanding that the words for numbers represent real objects. When children begin counting, they often repeat or skip numbers.

*Preschoolers* can count from one to three or up to about ten with improved accuracy. Learning one-to-one correspondence means they understand that the number name represents an exact amount. Preschoolers enjoy sorting and re-sorting objects based on their characteristics or ordering items by single characteristics such as "small" to "large." Children notice and imitate simple patterns.

*Older preschoolers and kindergartners* use more complex strategies to sort objects. They begin to understand that numerals represent quantities. Many four-year-olds can count to twenty with accuracy. The best way to help children learn math skills is through concrete experiences with everyday objects. Children are forming concepts of comparative math terms such as more than/less than, many/few, and big/small. They become interested in measurement and enjoy using these terms to estimate numbers, size, or weight.

## Questions for Teachers

- Are there things we can count in this book?

- Are there patterns in this book?

- Are there objects in this book that we can compare?

- Are there small objects in the book that we can gather and use for sorting, counting, and sequencing play (buttons, coins, etc.)?

## Sample Math Activities

### For Infants and Up

- Use fabrics with patterns (stripes, checks, or repeating objects) in your play areas: blankets, tablecloths, scarves.

- Provide a collection of objects from the book (toy animals, blocks, etc.) for children to play with. Provide different sizes of containers and tools for dump and fill play.

- Make simple matching games using stickers or pictures from the book on frozen juice concentrate lids or cardboard.

### For Toddlers and Up

- Use Duplos or wooden building blocks to build structures from the book.

- Count objects in the book's illustrations using felt pieces and using real objects.

- Prepare recipes with basic ingredients using simple directions. Have children count quantities together.

- Write recipes (ingredients, quantities, and steps) in the children's words after you prepare food.

- Have children help teachers do tasks that involve steps: setting the table, cleaning up, preparing for activities.

## For Preschoolers and Up

- Look for patterns in the book to explain what a pattern is. Look for patterns in real life. At circle time, have children predict the next step in a pattern.

- Have children count small objects from the book to match number cards.

- Use scales with counter toys and everyday objects to compare weights. Have children estimate weight.

- Use blocks or other classroom objects to measure how tall children are. Record results on a large graph.

- Make graphs of weather, opinions, or clothing characteristics (such as shoe color or short/long sleeves).

- Have children sort a collection using different characteristics. Have them brainstorm new ways to sort collections.

- Look for geometric shapes in the book. Have children find similar shapes in the classroom and outside.

- At circle time, do simple story problems based on the book. For example: "How many things did his little sister eat?"

- Have children draw maps of their bedrooms or houses. Have them make three-dimensional maps using blocks or small toys or pieces of paper.

## For Older Preschoolers and Kindergartners

● Have children estimate quantities of small items from the book. Help them develop strategies for estimating and see how accurate they are.

● Do whole-body math: have children solve story problems that involve counting body parts or children. Write the problems and solutions using math terms for children to see "+," "–," and "=" symbols in use.

● Draw maps of your school. Draw a map of the story. Have children find their streets on a map of your town. Have them map the way to the park, and walk it together.

# Science

In the early childhood classroom, science exploration should focus on basic scientific principles and general studies of earth and life science, since children's thinking is still very concrete. Earth science is all around them, from watching the seasons change to finding baby birds to watching plants grow. The scientific method—asking questions, experimenting, and drawing conclusions—mirrors children's instinctive explorations of their environment.

## Ages and Stages

*Infants and toddlers* experiment to see how objects behave and how they can manipulate them. Very young children do lots of oral exploration, so for safety's sake, put small objects (marbles, stones, feathers, etc.) inside clear plastic soda bottles and seal the lids with superglue or duct tape for safe exploration.

*Preschoolers* are very interested in characteristics of objects—they instinctively classify and sort as they make sense of their environment and attempt to gain control over it. Preschool children are very concrete thinkers and are most engaged by science concepts that they can see in action; for example, weather is more relevant than outer space. They begin to understand cause and effect and do simple testing of objects.

*Older preschoolers and kindergartners,* as their language and cooperative skills increase, are able to work together, form simple hypotheses, and examine results. Concepts should still be concrete and relevant to children's everyday experiences.

## Questions for Teachers

- Are there discoveries in this book? Are they purposeful or accidental?

- Does this book portray science in action—for example, life and death, plants and animals, weather, hypothesis testing?

- What do my students understand about the science portrayed in this book?

## Sample Science Activities

### For All Ages

- Compare objects: Are they alike or different? Use simple objects with younger children.

- Prepare foods from the book.

- Discuss the weather in the book.

- Bring smells and tastes from the book into the classroom.

### For Toddlers and Up

- Bring in natural objects from the books: stones, bones, leaves, plants, etc.

- Display them for children to touch and measure and draw.

- Hide them in a guessing box and let children feel them and guess what they are.

- Hide them in a paper bag and give clues so the kids can guess what they are.

- Have children dictate characteristics of the items.

- Provide artificial and natural building materials for any structures shown in the book.

## For Preschoolers and Up

- If the story features animal characters, read nonfiction books to learn facts about those animals.

- Set up "what will happen?" experiments. For example, "Will it float?" "Will it fit?" "Which weighs more?" Record the children's predictions and conclusions.

- Chart the weather for a week or two. Use descriptive words and pictures: cloudy, warm, cold, rainy, dry, etc.

- Group objects from the book by their characteristics. For example: food, plants, animals. Challenge children to find different ways to group them (for example, color, shape, size, purpose).

## For Older Preschoolers and Kindergartners

- Set up more complex "what will happen?" experiments that build on previous knowledge. For example, "Will it float if we put stones in it? Put air in it? Add corks?"

- Use field guides to identify the plants and birds around your center.

- Discuss climate and environments.

- Provide problem-solving science challenges that mirror problems in the book. For example, if in the story something breaks, you can design cases (using scrap materials) to cushion eggs and see how well they keep the eggs from breaking when they are dropped.

● Discuss what plants need in order to grow. Plant seeds and vary conditions to determine the best growing conditions for your seeds.

# Social Skills and Problem-Solving

It takes time for children to learn how to share space and materials. As they grow, they learn to cooperate, take turns, negotiate, and compromise. Try to ensure that several of your activities for each book have a social component.

## Ages and Stages

Major issues for *infants* include separation and emotional regulation. Toys that react help infants feel powerful and demonstrate cause and effect.

*Toddlers* experience separation anxiety to varying degrees and in conjunction with other stress. Independence versus dependence is a major theme as toddlers transition from "babies" to "big kids." Toddlers' emotional regulation varies widely among children and from day to day. Sharing and taking turns are the major developmental challenges with group play, so provide plenty of materials and space to support the parallel play toddlers prefer.

*Preschoolers* become more peer-focused than adult-focused, so they're motivated to change undesirable behaviors in order to play with other kids. Continuing issues include independence versus dependence, empathy, and emotional regulation. At around age three, children have a solid concept of ownership and are capable of empathy, or considering another person's point of view. Preschoolers enjoy practicing self-help skills but still need reminders and adult assistance as they rehearse.

*Older preschoolers and kindergartners* tend to become rule-oriented in an effort to feel control over their world. Four- and five-year-old children are still fairly egocentric, and they may attempt to bend rules in their own favor or exhibit rigid thinking about others' behavior. Exclusion and fairness are big themes with this age group.

## Questions for Teachers

- What are the social and emotional themes of this book? How do they relate to my children's developmental challenges?

- What kinds of problems are presented and solved in this book?

- What are some of the ways the characters display independence and self-reliance?

## Sample Activities Related to Social Skills and Problem-Solving

### For Infants

- Provide toys that require persistence (building blocks, puzzles, etc.), which help infants learn to manage frustration.

- Place interesting objects out of reach—on low shelves, under blankets, or inside of other toys—to make older infants work for them.

### For Toddlers and Up

- Book-based dramatic play kits encourage role-playing, turn-taking, and modeling.

- Puzzles encourage teamwork and problem-solving skills.

- Do cooking projects based on the book.

- Use pictures or drawings at interest centers to remind children of appropriate behavior and project directions.

## For Preschoolers and Up

- Classroom jobs such as setup, cleanup, and book chooser promote respect for materials, responsibility, and teamwork.

- After reading the book aloud, ask the children about the main character's struggles or problems. Brainstorm other solutions. Post these for parents.

- Build a fort, make a collage, or do other large-group projects.

- As a group, determine a few simple rules for classroom behavior. Have children help determine appropriate consequences. Post rules and reminders at trouble spots; for example, put up a sign saying "take one towel" on the paper towel dispenser.

## For Older Preschoolers and Kindergartners

- As a class, pick a community issue relating to your web that you'd like to do something about (for example, litter, children without mittens, graffiti). Brainstorm ideas for working on the problem. Determine the steps you'll take, implement a plan, and summarize your results on a bulletin board and/or in the newsletter.

- Reorganize an interest area in your classroom to stage an activity relating to your web. Have the kids make suggestions, gather materials, and present the activity to visitors.

# Troubleshooting

Experienced teachers know that even the best-laid plans can go astray and any change to teaching and planning approaches can require new classroom management. The following situations describe stumbling blocks you may encounter as you shift to more open-ended activities and book-based webbing.

## Fighting

If infants and toddlers are getting frustrated about sharing toys, you may not have enough materials. Provide one of the "most desirable" item—for example, baby dolls or telephones—for each child. Make sure that you have at least two fun choices for each child in your group. Redirection and modeling (playing alongside them) help very young children share space and materials. Remind preschoolers of turn-taking strategies, and use a timer if necessary.

## Hoarding

Young children in particular may become so in love with a particular activity or set of toys that they don't want to share it with anyone. See if your program has a way to allow a passionate child to have unlimited access to her favorites. For example, you might allow her to play quietly alone during snack time or take a few of the objects to her nap mat for one-on-one time. The other children can accept this if teachers explain that it is very important to the child and that they, too, can have undivided toy time when they really need it. If you can't make this work in your group, let hoarders choose which toys they'll share. When you empower them to be part of the decision, most children will give up some toys rather than have them taken away. If an item or activity is simply too contentious, set it aside for a later date.

## Chaos

If the activities you're planning all require an adult presence, they may not be developmentally appropriate. Try scaling them down or reducing them to their elements, so that children can master one step at a time.

# Crowding

If all the children clump up at one or two centers, you may need to allow more room for those activities. You may also need to spice up the other activities in the room. Preschool children can understand group size limits, so if you post the number of children who can play in each area, that will help. If children don't move on their own, you can redirect them when play is no longer productive (they begin using materials inappropriately, etc.). Or you can set time limits for children to rotate in and out of a particular spot. This last option isn't ideal because it doesn't allow children to become engrossed. Teachers facing this situation should rethink the layout of the room and plan to provide more time and space for popular activities. Try to determine the most appealing elements of the popular activity, and then incorporate them into other areas of the room.

# Milling

If children move from area to area without becoming engaged, the activities may not be challenging enough, or they may be too challenging. They might also require too much adult facilitation. Reduce the amount of teacher direction, and increase the variety of challenges.

# Bouncing

If children move quickly between activities even though they appear interested and engaged, you may have too many things going on at once. Try reducing the number and scope of activities.

# Quitting

If children appear to be exhausting the interest centers too quickly—not spending much time at each or using materials inappropriately—you may not have planned enough. Add an interest area or two, and try making the ones you have more complex. Use children's invented activities to guide your choices.

# Whining

If many children are demanding teacher assistance, the directions may not be clear, or the projects may be too complicated. For special events, ask a parent volunteer to help out with a challenging area. Before you open the interest centers for play, give a tour of all of them, and explain the possibilities at each. In all your areas, leave picture directions of the things you hope the children will do—photos of kids cutting, etc. Encourage children to take turns being helpers in different spots.

# But What Are They Learning?

Another challenge when planning open-ended curriculum is helping staff and parents understand the learning outcomes of what may look like "only" play. There's a lot of curricular overlap with book-based planning; below are just a few of the ways that the activities suggested earlier involve several kinds of learning. (Chapter 4 has more suggestions for introducing the entire book-based approach to staff and parents.) On an ongoing basis, posting the following list will help you convey the value of play-based learning:

- *Recipes* involve math (counting, measuring, fractions), science (properties of matter, transformation, nutrition), and sensory discrimination (taste, texture, sounds).

- *Storytelling and retelling* (felt boards, storyboards, and dictation) involve counting and sequencing, fine motor skills, and creative arts.

- *Art projects* involve art appreciation, fine motor skills (coordination), gross motor skills (with larger scale projects), sensory play (tactile exploration of materials), math and pre-reading skills such as sequencing and ordering, and language arts (illustrating a story).

- *Music play* incorporates art appreciation, listening skills, sensory discrimination, math (finding/matching rhythms), and gross motor skills.

- *Sensory play* involves math (quantifying, measuring), science (properties of matter), fine motor coordination, gross motor skills (with outdoor sensory play in water, sand, etc.), and language arts (vocabulary building).

- *Dramatic play* involves problem-solving, creative expression, and language arts skills (conversation, vocabulary building, and sequencing).

- *Fine motor play* with manipulatives such as blocks, Lego building blocks, and counters involves math (one-to-one correspondence, counting, quantifying), problem-solving (building, puzzle play), and social skills (cooperation, sharing, and turn-taking).

# Looking Ahead

Thoughtful planning and developmentally appropriate, open-ended activities will help your book-based webs engage and inspire children and teachers. As you implement your ideas, you're likely to take note of things that worked well and things that didn't. Setting up systems to document your work in advance will help you stay focused on activities as they happen. Chapter 3 will help you gather feedback as you go, evaluate activities after the fact, and organize all this information to make it accessible for further use with parents and staff.

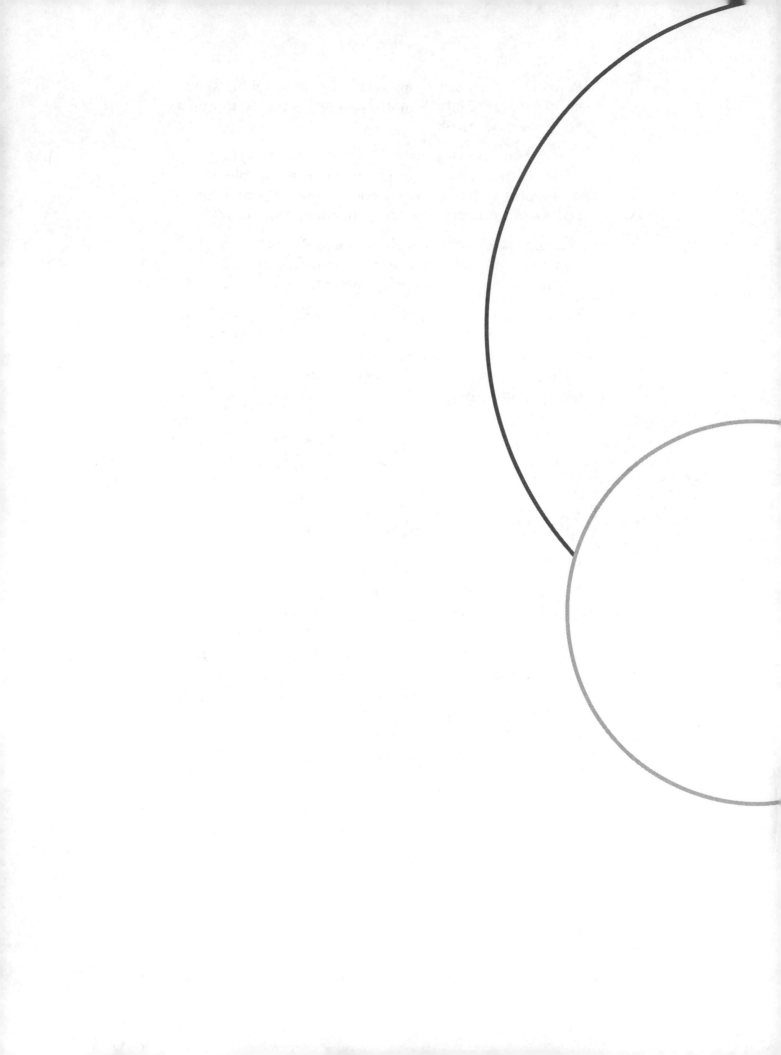

# 3 Documentation and Evaluation

Although a working web may look quite messy, thoughtful planning goes into each unit. As you work through the activities you've planned, take notes as you go. Ideas that initially seem unmanageable can often be reworked. Careful documentation of your webs will make them useful in three ways: to help staff with future planning, to document individual children's development, and to communicate to parents and the community the important work that children do every day as they play.

# What to Keep and How to Keep It

Because emergent curriculum responds to children and teachers, a book web can change dramatically from group to group. Don't save everything from each web with the idea that it should be done exactly the same way the next time. Do save "base" items: things that can be used in many different ways and examples to teach new staff about the process. You'll be storing these items in three locations: classroom files (organized by book title); children's portfolio files (sorted by child's name, within each class), and teacher portfolio files.

## Classroom Files

Organize your classroom planning files by book title. This section covers some of the items to save for each unit.

Completed webs are a good reference for further units with the same children, or for similar units with different children and staff. Jot down brief notes about things that worked well or didn't. On the next page is an example of a completed planning web for toddlers.

Compiled webs are documents rather than drawings. Group activities by interest area. If you have time, list the learning/conceptual outcomes for each activity. Post this on your parent board, send copies home to parents, or do both. You'll notice that in the following compiled web, some of the planned activities for

# Toddler Book Web Example

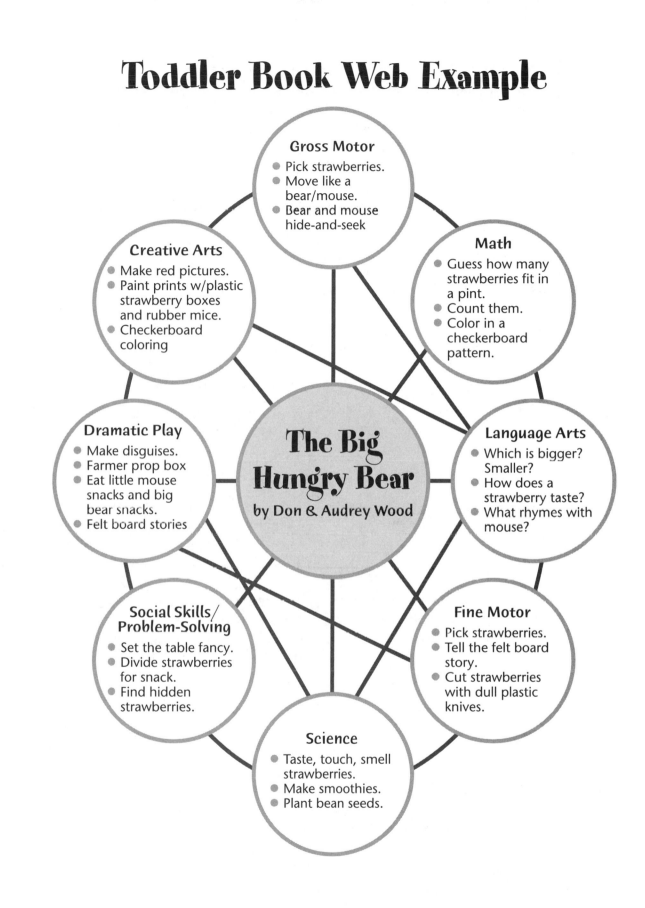

**Gross Motor**
- Pick strawberries.
- Move like a bear/mouse.
- Bear and mouse hide-and-seek

**Math**
- Guess how many strawberries fit in a pint.
- Count them.
- Color in a checkerboard pattern.

**Creative Arts**
- Make red pictures.
- Paint prints w/plastic strawberry boxes and rubber mice.
- Checkerboard coloring

**Dramatic Play**
- Make disguises.
- Farmer prop box
- Eat little mouse snacks and big bear snacks.
- Felt board stories

**The Big Hungry Bear**
by Don & Audrey Wood

**Language Arts**
- Which is bigger? Smaller?
- How does a strawberry taste?
- What rhymes with mouse?

**Social Skills/ Problem-Solving**
- Set the table fancy.
- Divide strawberries for snack.
- Find hidden strawberries.

**Fine Motor**
- Pick strawberries.
- Tell the felt board story.
- Cut strawberries with dull plastic knives.

**Science**
- Taste, touch, smell strawberries.
- Make smoothies.
- Plant bean seeds.

*The Little Mouse* didn't actually happen, and new ones were added. This is what happens when teachers allow curriculum to emerge.

Below is a sample letter sent to parents of toddlers with information about the compiled web related to *The Little Mouse, the Red Ripe Strawberry, and the Big Hungry Bear.*

Dear Toddler Parents,

Look at all the fun we had with this classic book! The notes in parentheses indicate some of the learning outcomes for each activity. Use this list to start conversations with your child or plan fun things to do at home.

### Creative Arts

Make felt board pieces for kids to tell the story in their own words. (repetition, sequencing, articulation)

Play with the farmer/gardening prop box. (science, cooperation)

Make "red" art using a variety of media. (vocabulary and science)

Figure out which colors you get when you blend red with blue, yellow, white. (science)

### Language Arts

Taste strawberries. Are they sweet? sour? chewy? soft? wet? dry? (vocabulary, articulation, print awareness, plus science/classification)

Ask: Which one is bigger, a mouse or a bear? Which one is longer, a spoon or a ladder? Which one is taller, a tree or a bear? (comparative vocabulary)

Ask the kids to describe how to make smoothies. Write down the recipe in their words. (description, recall, synthesis, sequencing)

Look for objects that begin with "l" (little), "m" (mouse) "h" (hungry), "b" (bear), and "s" (strawberry). Make letter collages. (phonics, creative arts, fine muscle control)

Make lists of words that rhyme with "bear" and "mouse." (phonemic awareness)

### Science

Taste other fruits, and classify each as sweet or sour. Find things that are red. (classification)

Make strawberry smoothies with vanilla yogurt and mashed strawberries. (nutrition, properties of matter)

Put scents on cotton balls: strawberry, lemon, cinnamon, vanilla. Have children describe the smells. (discrimination, classification)

Save fruit waste to start a compost bin. (life cycle)

Plant beans and watch them grow. (life cycle)

## Math

Using the answers about fruits, make a graph to show how many fruits are sweet and how many are sour. (one-to-one correspondence, representing quantities)

Guess how many strawberries fit in a box; then count to see how many actually do. (estimation, one-to-one correspondence, volume)

Using checkerboard fabric like the mouse's tablecloth, count the squares in different sections. See what other shapes you can make by arranging string on top of the checkerboard. (patterns, geometry)

## Social Skills and Problem-Solving

Play hide-and-seek. Have hiders be the mice and finders be the bears.

Go on a strawberry hunt. Have a teacher hide "strawberries" (red balls or felt pieces), and have everyone hunt to find them. (teamwork, gross motor activity)

## Fine Motor

Pick strawberries. (gross motor in bending to find the strawberries on the plants, holding leaves aside, not stepping on plants in the rows, science)

Tell the felt board story. (sequencing, articulation)

Cut strawberries and bananas with dull plastic knives. (hand-eye coordination, math, social skills)

## Gross Motor

Play bear and mouse hide-and-seek. (problem-solving, dramatic play)

Pick strawberries. (fine motor coordination to pluck the berry without pulling up the plant, science, cooperation)

## Dramatic Play

Make disguises. (performance arts)

Tell the story with felt pieces. (hand-eye coordination, articulation, sequencing)

Here are some other items to save for each unit:

- lists of related books (including books from the library)

- shopping lists for any consumable items needed

- the requested donations list that you give parents at the beginning of the unit

- dictation summaries, such as children's responses to questions, graphs, and recipes. Post these during the unit, and then include them in the book file. Teachers may opt to copy some of these for their portfolios. These also make interesting newsletter fillers.

- a few typical examples of individual children's work for each book, which will help illustrate this approach when training staff or doing parent workshops

## Children's Files

If your program uses a portfolio approach to track children's development, photocopy illustrative samples of children's writing and art, take snapshots of bigger projects or the children in action, and include copies of group lists, etc., that each child participates in. If your program does not use portfolios, consider saving a few special examples of each child's work—items that display special interests and particular skills. Date the work in an unobtrusive spot because parents often save these as keepsakes.

Snapshots of children's work show individual development and preserve images of creations that are not permanent—block structures, sidewalk art, or costumes and performances. These snapshots can also be used on an educational bulletin board or in permanent displays around the classroom to help parents and new staff understand the kinds of learning that take place. Photographs of real kids can also inspire children as they play. Include photos of small groups and individuals to illustrate competence and creativity in teachers' professional portfolios.

Programs have several options for taking photographs of children at work. *Digital cameras* are handy for several reasons: you can check the photo on the spot, you can delete poor shots, you only print the photos you need, and it's easy to e-mail them to parents as well as store photos long term. Another option is to use traditional film cameras. Local film developers may offer a bulk discount, but developing costs can quickly add up, so be sure to discuss in advance how many and what kinds of photos you'll be taking. *Instant cameras* are the least cost-effective way to document classroom work, but they can provide occasional instant gratification: they can show that a new child who's having rough drop-offs becomes engrossed during the day; they can capture scenes that might disappear quickly, like a towering pile of bricks; they can document major milestones so the child can take the picture home that day to share with the family.

*Videotapes* are another great way to document the work you do with children and allow parents to see how their child interacts with others when the parents are not present. You can also videotape dramatic performances. You can play the tapes during potlucks and open houses. Many families have video cameras that they may be willing to loan to programs, or they might volunteer to videotape the children on occasion. Some school districts have video cameras available for use in the classroom, or you can rent one from some specialty video/camera stores. As with cameras, digital videos make editing, copying, and storage a breeze.

Consider recording *audiotapes* with a simple handheld recorder. Tapes of storytelling and circle time can be replayed during rest period. Tapes of individual children explaining their work or singing and playing together are a nice item to include in portfolios. And general tapes of the classroom at work can help teachers identify problems and refine their teaching techniques. Audiotapes are relatively inexpensive in bulk; as many people convert to digital media, cassette tapes are also a good item to seek as donations from businesses or families.

# Parent and Community Education

Before you store all your materials for future reference, you can use them to convey the importance of children's play and encourage literacy in your community. Here are a few ways to spread the news.

Designate a bulletin board to feature book-related activities. Include dictated lists, story samples, artwork, compiled webs, and brief explanations of the importance of each kind of work. Besides keeping current families informed, this will be an informative snapshot of your program for visitors—prospective families, staff, and community members.

Reserve space in your newsletter to highlight curriculum. (Send the newsletter to prospective families as well as currently enrolled ones.)

Occasionally send an explanatory note home with art projects to explain the skills involved. For example, "This is a letter collage. The children were looking for pictures of things that begin with 'b.' This promotes *phonemic awareness,* which is an understanding of the distinct sounds that make up words, and *phonics,* the awareness that different letters make particular sounds. This activity also involves fine motor coordination, as children cut or tear and glue the pictures; composition, as they sort and arrange items on the page; and teamwork, as they confer with others. You may notice that some pictures don't appear to begin with 'b.' We expect children to make mistakes as they learn this skill (for example, they might hear a 'b' elsewhere in the word or confuse 'b' with 'p'), but sometimes they are using another word to describe the picture, as in 'box' instead of 'gift.'"

If your center sends home daily or weekly notes for individual children, use these to point out how your programming responds to and supports each child's development. For example, "We have been reading books about construction, and Emma has been building things during interest center time. She sorts all the blocks by shape and size before she uses them. This is a pre-reading skill."

If you have a Web site, reserve a page to feature special projects. Use captions to explain the educational basis for what's happening in the picture. (Be sure to obtain permission from families before posting their children's photos online.)

Display children's artwork several times a year at local businesses. Some times to consider: Reading Month (March), the Month of the Young Child (April), Book Week (November).

Present community workshops on the importance of play and the value of books. Encourage parents to read to their children regularly. Give workshop attendees guidelines to help them select quality books and ideas to extend the books they read at home.

# Evaluation

Book-based webbing shouldn't be an endurance sport. While staff should mine a book for all its useful elements, a book unit shouldn't continue after children's interest has waned. The ultimate evaluation for a book-based unit is not how long it lasts, but the level of engagement and interest children show. How can staff and parents be confident that book-based webs are meeting children's intellectual and emotional needs? Teachers can gather feedback from three sources: children, staff, and parents.

# Children

At the end of the unit, reread the book, and ask the children what it was about. Some children will summarize plot; some will discuss themes; some will focus on one character. All are meaningful ways to read and process books.

To identify concrete learning outcomes, ask the children what they learned from various activities. Use open-ended phrases such as "What do we know about birds?" and "Do we have any more questions about birds?" Avoid yes/no questions, which discourage elaboration. Have one teacher record or take notes during this discussion.

These are some general cues that a book was appropriately engaging:

- Children ask to read other books on any subject.

- Children are animated when they discuss it.

- Most of the children in the room have an opinion on the book. They don't have to like the book—articulating criticism is a valuable academic and social skill.

- Children see and describe connections across the activities. You might hear them discussing scenes from the book in the dramatic play area, or building structures from the story in the block area, or looking for nature elements of the story during outside time.

# Staff

At the end of the unit, be sure to gather and discuss feedback from your team members. At your planning meetings, ask each staff member to choose a favorite aspect and a least favorite aspect of the book unit. Have them explain why. Ask each teacher to make at least one suggestion for the next unit and one suggestion for future use of the same book. (File the notes from this meeting in your book folder.) Have the person responsible for curriculum oversight (director or program director) drop by your meeting to offer his or her perspective on the work you're doing.

Revisit specific goals for the children. Discuss evidence that the unit contributes something positive toward a goal. Note areas for improvement. When you compile your completed webs into a written document (see previous example for *The Little Mouse;* more examples for all ages are in Chapter 4), note the educational outcomes. This will help staff focus on teachable moments and articulate learning outcomes to parents, and it will help parents understand the academic value of hands-on, play-based learning.

## Parents

Parents have a unique perspective on what happens in the classroom. They see the end results in artwork or photographs; they note the classroom climate and activities at drop-off and pickup; they hear their child talk about meaningful themes and activities in conversations and play choices at home. Encourage parents to share their observations about each unit. Because daily communications are usually devoted to immediate needs, it may be more convenient for parents to send comments via e-mail or in a written note. On your parent bulletin board, designate a spot for brief comments. Headings such as "We Loved It. We Want More!" and "Next Time, Consider: _____" will invite positive comments and concrete criticism where appropriate. Posting this will give all parents a broader view of your program and their children's experiences in it.

## Looking Ahead

Careful documentation and thoughtful evaluation are a critical aspect of book-webbing. They provide a record of children's individual development and group dynamics, they assist future planning and staff training, and they help teachers convey to parents and community members the educational value of play. Teachers who do dynamic webs but neglect to record and analyze results will sell themselves short and, in the long run, make webbing less effective. If you're overwhelmed or disorganized with your first few webs, at least do the basics: photos, compiled webs, and bulletin board displays. As you become familiar with the process, you can establish systems to help you gather and utilize all the wonderful results of your planning. If you are the first member of your teaching team to suggest doing book-based webbing, Chapter 4 will help you explain book-based webbing in a dynamic and easy-to-use workshop. It will also help you explain the process to parents and let them know how the changes will affect their child and what they see at the center.

# Reference

Wood, Don and Audrey. 1990. *The little mouse, the red ripe strawberry, and the big hungry bear.* New York: Child's Play International.

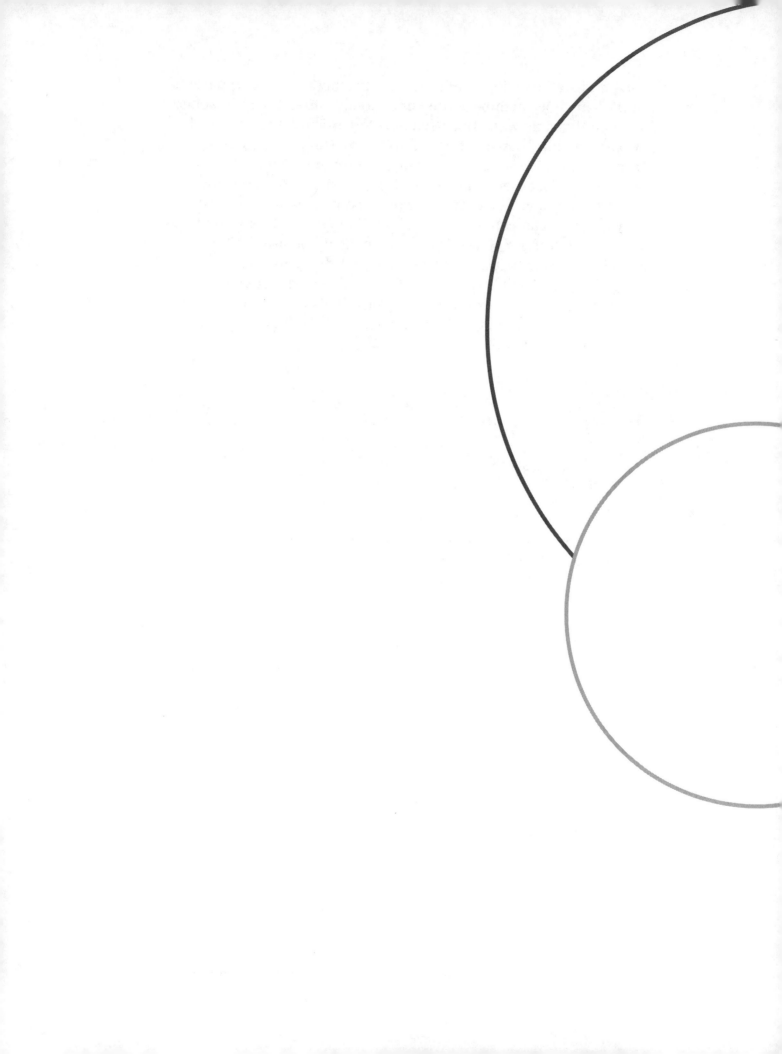

# 4

# Introducing Book-Based Webbing to Staff and Families

*After observing her students' reading habits for several days in preparation for her first book-based web, preschool teacher Megan V. realized her students' favorite was* How Do Dinosaurs Say Good Night? *by Jane Yolen. It's a rhyming text of about 150 words.*

*"I thought to myself, 'This will never work!'" Megan said. "I was a little disappointed because it is such a simple book. I didn't think there would be much I could do with it. But when I started actually going through the pages and thinking about different interest areas, I came up with a lot of activities."*

*After discussing her ideas with colleagues and parents, Megan got even more suggestions. Her first web's activities lasted several weeks, to the surprise and delight of children, staff, and parents. They ended the unit with an exclamation point: a field trip to the Museum of Natural History to look at real dinosaur skeletons and displays.*

Megan is an educated teacher with several years' classroom experience. She liked the idea of book-based webbing and recognized the educational foundation for planning curriculum this way. But when she tried to choose a book that her children loved, her confidence faltered. To get over that hurdle, she reminded herself of the potential payoff of making books more central in the classroom. She also asked for help. In this chapter, I'll discuss ways to introduce this approach to staff and parents and offer suggestions for clearing the hurdles along the way.

# Introducing Book-Based Curriculum Webbing to Teachers

The first questions you're likely to hear when you propose a change in curriculum or routine are universal: "How much work does it involve?" and "Why should we bother?" Adult learners are not so different from child learners: they learn by doing.

Rather than overwhelming them with papers and studies and all the technical information, capture their interest by showing them firsthand how much books have to offer.

Before your next staff meeting or in-service, choose a really great picture book that you'll web with the staff. Jot down some ideas for activities. (Having a few notes will help you get the ball rolling if people are unclear on the concept or resistant to offering suggestions.) At the meeting, walk the teachers through a web much as you want them to walk their classrooms through a web. Ask that teachers participate in the exercise as though they are members of a class. The more relaxed and fun the atmosphere, the more creative your participants will be.

## Start with the Book

Hold it up and ask if anyone has any ideas what the book might be about. Read it aloud. Review: ask the teachers to describe the story line, conflict, etc.

## Begin with a Brainstorm

Have one staff member take notes on a newsprint tablet or chalkboard. Pose questions one at a time: "Is there math in this book?" As people share ideas, others will be inspired to jump in. Move on to other interest areas: "What are some language arts activities that would work well with this text?" and "Can you see science in this book?"

## Show Them What a Book-Based Web Looks Like

On a clean sheet, draw a web using the ideas suggested during brainstorming. Make your big announcement: "This is a book-based web, and this is how we'd like you to start thinking about planning." You may also want to hand out copies of the completed book-based webs found later in this chapter.

# Briefly Explain the Benefits of Planning This Way

- It makes books the center of the curriculum, rather than a side note.

- Books provide a meaningful framework for children to make connections across interest areas and between the things they read and the things they see in the world around them.

- This approach encourages parent participation while emphasizing the importance of literacy.

- Webbing makes books come alive and gets kids excited about reading even before they can read themselves.

# Make a Timeline for Your Program to Do a Trial Run

Using the guidelines in Chapter 1, sketch out a plan to accomplish a book-based web. Include an informal parent meeting to introduce the concept and invite participation. The kinds of adjustments and time required to achieve them will depend on the kind of planning your program currently does.

If your program already uses emergent curriculum and curriculum webbing, this transition will be minor. The biggest change will be starting with a book rather than starting with a concept or theme, so you may need time to evaluate your library and acquire new books.

If your program uses linear, fill-in-the-blank planning, you may need to ease into the new format. Experienced teachers may need time to feel confident that webbing will address their curricular goals. One way to facilitate that transition is to start slowly: set aside an afternoon per week or an hour every day to do book-based activities on a smaller scale. Set a goal to work up to an entire book-based unit within a specific amount of time, depending on your staff's skills and classroom situations.

If your program currently uses preplanned units, your staff may be more comfortable modifying an existing unit as a trial run. You might, for example, take a unit such as "The Life Cycle" and pair it with *The Very Hungry Caterpillar* (Carle 1969). Adapting existing activities to make them more relevant to a particular book can help teachers better understand the process. Your staff may also want to plan units themselves without much input from children during the first few webs, just to see if it will really work. Given time to iron out the wrinkles, teachers will soon see that books are a wonderful foundation for all kinds of learning units. If they run into resistance from the children or if activities flop, it may be because they've left the children out of the planning process. Children are more likely to try new foods if they help prepare them because they've invested something in the meal. Soliciting children's input will also help staff address their particular interests and needs, making activities more relevant and engaging. Revisit the troubleshooting section of Chapter 2.

If book-based webbing appeals to staff, but the thought of implementing such a big change is overwhelming, break the task down into manageable goals. For programs in a state of transition, focusing on one element may be the best they can do—for example, evaluating and building the classroom library, observing children's interests, or planning open-ended activities. Instead of making a giant leap, plan simple steps in the right direction.

# What's in It for Me?

Staff resistance to change stems from a variety of sources. Some teachers have been in the classroom so long that they've settled comfortably into their routines. To get them out of their comfort zone, encourage them to start with something familiar—a best-loved book, a book relating to one of their favorite themes, or activities for which they have a lot of existing classroom materials. Less-experienced staff may lack the confidence in new methods or in their own skills to develop new activities. Supervisors can try two strategies to battle resistance: divide and conquer or rally the troops. To divide and conquer staff, pair experienced and/or enthused teachers with staff who are less so. To rally the troops, allow the teachers who are excited about the new approach to work together. Other teachers can observe their successes. Later, the successful book-web teachers can mentor the reluctant ones. Program directors can also go into the classrooms of reluctant teachers to model successful webbing activities.

It's always helpful for a trainer or leader to be prepared for the curveball questions from resistant staff. Here are some frequently asked questions (or comments) and suggested responses:

Q: Isn't this the same as theme-based planning, after all?

A: It's true that the book creates themes for planning. But these will vary from group to group. The benefit of starting with a book rather than a theme is that you are following children's interests rather than making assumptions about them. A good book can have any number of themes ripe for exploration.

Q: Isn't that a lot more work?

A: Whether you currently have a relatively structured environment or a more creative, spontaneous classroom, you're already doing curriculum with children. As opposed to plugging unrelated activities into a grid, this kind of planning is more fluid because activities are naturally and logically related. The book provides a beacon to guide your planning.

Q: What if my kids pick hard books?

A: First, ensure that your classroom library is stocked with quality literature (see Chapter 6 for specifics). Besides stocking strong books, get rid of the fluff books. Television-themed books are always popular, but they're little more than advertisements or recaps of popular shows and movies. If you're having trouble with a good book your class loves, get the children on board during the planning. Children are especially good at thinking outside the box. What is it about the book that they find attractive? Use that angle to find interesting and appropriate activities.

Q:  I tried this, and the kids didn't go for it.

A:  Perhaps the activities you chose were all book-related, but not open-ended. Have you asked an outside observer for input? Keep in mind that even in the hands of a skilled, experienced teacher, every book web may not be a rousing success. Pause to reflect on why the web failed, and then learn from the mistakes and move on.

# Stumbling Blocks for Staff

If teachers have problems implementing a new program, here are a few sticking points to consider.

*Time*  Learning a new way to do something will take more time in the beginning. Be sure that teachers have time for meetings and extra time for planning. Be creative: challenge the staff to find time in the day; multitask; ask parents to help out in the rooms; hire a support teacher temporarily, if necessary.

*Money*  If you don't have all the materials you need to do the activities you'd like, use some of the suggestions in Chapter 6 (Building a Classroom Library) to economize. Hold a dedicated fund-raiser. Seek donations from the community. Challenge staff to see what they can do with the resources they have.

*Technique*  Some staff may need to adjust teaching styles with this approach. Have teachers observe each other and make suggestions; at the very least, have a supervisor observe and model in the classroom.

*Incentives*  Encouraging words, recognition of effort or achievement, and creative awards are easy ways to let staff know that their efforts matter. Something as simple as kudos in the newsletter or a personal note of thanks can be a big motivator. Encourage staff who embrace the new approach and master book-based webbing to present the idea to their peers at local early childhood conferences.

# Getting Parents on Board

Invite parents to take this book-based web journey with you. It will alert them to potential rough spots as you incorporate changes in your program, it will convey that you value their input and participation, and it will enrich the activities you do if parents share their individual skills and resources.

The idea of change is often more overwhelming than the actual process. Making time for a preview meeting invites parents to voice concerns and make suggestions face-to-face. An informal meeting similar to the one you'll hold for staff will help parents understand the scope of the new approach as well as the benefits. Providing child care or refreshments or both is a way to increase parent participation, but don't be disappointed if only a few families turn out. They will communicate what they learn to other parents and may turn out to be advocates for the new program. Parents don't really need to do anything with their children in relation to this change besides be aware of it, so sending home a letter will be adequate notice. If you can't make time for a meeting until you've done a web or two, a letter such as the following example is a good introduction.

Dear Parents,

We're excited about trying a new approach to curriculum called "Book-Based Webbing," and we want to share it with you.

Rather than building our curriculum around a theme ("transportation," "colors," etc.), we're going to start with a great book and pull themes, concepts, and activities from the book itself. We feel this will benefit the children in several ways:

- We'll choose books the children love.
- The context of story helps make ideas and concepts concrete, meaningful, and engaging for young children.
- We'll help children make connections across the curriculum, preparing them to be active learners in elementary school and beyond.

Many of you have skills that can help us with our webbing. At the bottom of this page, please list any talents you'd like to share and return it to us. We'll let you know when we have specific needs. We'll send a note home when we introduce each new book and post our plans with a list of needs on the parent bulletin boards.

Our first book will be [INSERT TITLE AND AUTHOR HERE]. We'll be posting pictures and notes about our progress to help you better understand the process. We look forward to your comments and suggestions!

Your partners in education,

[INSERT STAFF NAMES HERE]

parent's name:                     phone number:                    e-mail address:

skills you can share:

The next letter is a model for one you will send home with each unit:

---

Dear Parents,

We'll be building our next book web around [INSERT TITLE AND AUTHOR]. As we begin gathering materials and planning activities, we'd like to invite you to participate in various aspects of this unit.

If you've never read this book, please do! There is a copy on our sign-in table that you can read while at the center; please don't remove it from the premises. The book is also available at the public library and local bookstores.

Some of the themes and concepts featured in this book include: [INSERT HERE]. If you have any activity ideas, we'd love to hear them. If you have a skill or family tradition that relates to this book, please speak to us about a classroom visit.

We are also looking for some loans or donations of materials to supplement our interest areas. If you have any of the following available, please let us know. We'll need these items by [INSERT DATE]. Please label any items you would like returned. [INSERT LIST OF ITEMS HERE; NOTE IF THEY CANNOT BE RETURNED].

We estimate that activities relating to this book will take us through [INSERT DATE]. If you have responses, suggestions, or donations, please write us a note or send us an e-mail. We'd love to talk with you about these things at drop-off and pickup, but sometimes families have more pressing concerns at those times of day.

As always, we thank you for your time and efforts.
[INSERT STAFF NAMES HERE]

---

# Frequently Asked Questions from Parents

Parents are most interested in their own child's comfort and development. Their concerns about the change are likely to be very different from teachers'.

Q: What will this mean for my child?

A: All good things! Your child is likely to demonstrate an increased interest in reading; you may notice him or her "webbing" or brainstorming activity ideas about the books you read. If you don't already read aloud to your child every day, this is a great time to establish the habit. You might even scan your own or library bookshelves for other books related to our topics. Because we're inviting parent participation in these projects, your child may expect to see you at the center in some capacity when he or she sees other parents joining us from time to time. If your schedule doesn't allow midday participation, consider making or gathering materials at home so your child can see your investment in the activities he or she does at the center.

Q: How will I know what my child is learning?

A: When we finish a book web, we'll compile our activities into a list by age group. After each web is completed, we'll try to note educational outcomes. If you ever have questions about the educational value of a particular activity, please ask, and we'll explain. What looks like play is actually important work. (Use web examples for each age group starting on page 74 to show them what you mean.)

Q: My child is especially good at [math, science, etc.]. Won't all this emphasis on books give him short shrift?

A: Actually, the book is just a starting point—a springboard for other activities. It's not a limiting factor, but a means of extending interest and play. Children learn best by doing: they need concrete, hands-on experiences to internalize their observations about math, science, and other subjects. Linking all the activities to a book helps them make connections among interest areas so it broadens their knowledge base about each. A book-based program also promotes reading skills, which are necessary for academic success in any discipline.

# Share Your Plans (and Excitement!) with Children

Adult enthusiasm about any approach to learning is contagious. Children don't need to know why you're reformatting planning; they just need to know that any changes they notice are going to be fun. You don't even need to say, "We're going to start planning with books because reading is important." The very act of placing a book at the center of your web implies that it is.

# Tying It All Together: Book Web Examples

The following examples of webs for each age group have two components: the graphic or planning version of the web and the text summary of activities that actually happened. Teachers can share and discuss these examples with staff and parents to help them understand the dynamic nature of webbing.

You'll see that the webs and the text summary don't match exactly. This is typical with emergent curriculum. To allow more time for the most engaging activities, teachers may need to omit other things they have planned. Or, once they begin implementing a web, teachers may omit or modify plans that are impractical for various reasons, ranging from external factors such as weather or availability of materials to internal factors including children's moods and developmental concerns.

## Infant and Young Toddler Book Web

*The Very Hungry Caterpillar* (Carle 1969)

In this web, notice that the Math bubble on the graphic web disappeared completely from the text web, and sensory play was added to the text version. When the teachers tried to compare

# Infant and Young Toddler Book Web

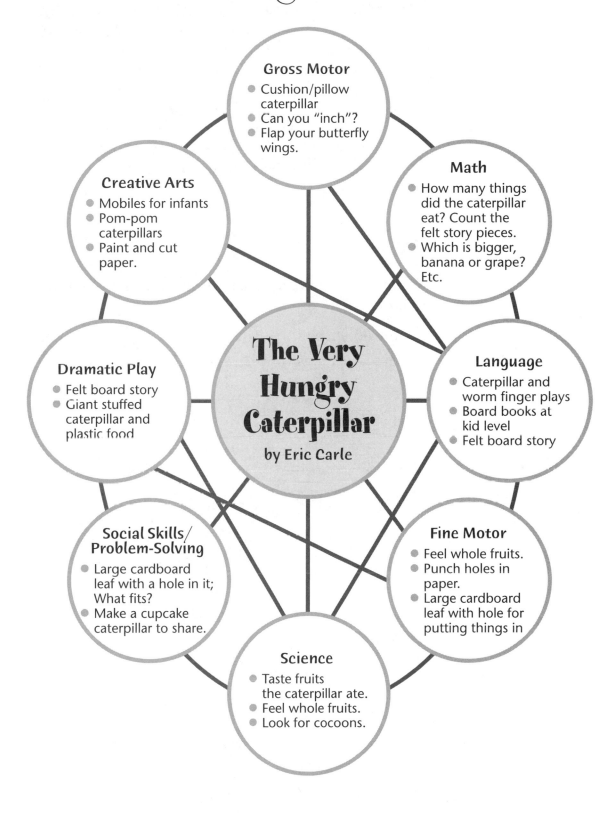

**Gross Motor**
- Cushion/pillow caterpillar
- Can you "inch"?
- Flap your butterfly wings.

**Creative Arts**
- Mobiles for infants
- Pom-pom caterpillars
- Paint and cut paper.

**Math**
- How many things did the caterpillar eat? Count the felt story pieces.
- Which is bigger, banana or grape? Etc.

**Dramatic Play**
- Felt board story
- Giant stuffed caterpillar and plastic food

## The Very Hungry Caterpillar
### by Eric Carle

**Language**
- Caterpillar and worm finger plays
- Board books at kid level
- Felt board story

**Social Skills/ Problem-Solving**
- Large cardboard leaf with a hole in it; What fits?
- Make a cupcake caterpillar to share.

**Fine Motor**
- Feel whole fruits.
- Punch holes in paper.
- Large cardboard leaf with hole for putting things in

**Science**
- Taste fruits the caterpillar ate.
- Feel whole fruits.
- Look for cocoons.

the sizes of plastic fruit with the toddlers, they realized the young group was doing more oral exploration of the plastic fruit than they were talking about them. The teachers responded by first allowing children to examine real fruit, then preparing and serving it for them to taste. With the felt story pieces, the children primarily wanted to play with the pieces and tell lines from the story. The teachers added cotton balls and leaves to the sensory table to give the children the chance to manipulate and explore their textures as well as rehearse a line from the book, "In the light of the moon, a little egg lay on a leaf." The quantity of cotton balls in the table gave the older toddlers something to count, if they wanted to.

## Sensory Play

- Taste fruits (mashed for young infants, mashed or grated for older ones).

- Examine whole fruits.

- Play with cotton balls and felt leaves in a large plastic tub.

## Language Arts

- Do finger plays. For example:

"The Caterpillar"

Roly-poly caterpillar
Into a corner crept
Spun himself a blanket
Then for a long time slept.
Roly-poly caterpillar
Wakened by and by
Found himself with
    beautiful wings
He was a butterfly!

"The Worm"

In the corner of our garden
Where the earth is very
    firm,
Underneath a little stone,
There lives a great big
    worm!

- Put extra copies of *The Very Hungry Caterpillar* board books on the kid shelves.

- Tell a felt board story of *The Very Hungry Caterpillar*.

## Gross Motor

- Make a cushion caterpillar for climbing on.
- Play with a nylon tunnel: put toys inside.

## Fine Motor

- Pick up cotton balls and put them in containers.
- Cut a hole in a large cardboard leaf and let babies feed things through it.
- Put fruit stickers on frozen juice concentrate lids for children to sort.

## Creative Arts

- Paint in a plastic swimming pool using cornstarch paint. Make bulletin board with Eric Carle–style art using pages painted by kids.
- Teachers make a butterfly mobile to hang in infant room.
- Teachers make a fruit mobile to hang in infant room.
- Teachers paint caterpillars on the window ledge in infant room.
- Toddlers: glue pom-poms together to make caterpillars.

## Science

- Toddlers: taste the fruit. Is it sweet or sour? Make separate piles of sweet and sour.
- Toddlers: Which are bigger: strawberries, blueberries, pears, or plums?

## Dramatic Play

- Use felt board pieces to tell the story.
- Tell the story with a stuffed caterpillar and plastic food; leave these in a basket for free play.

# Toddler Book Web

*The Runaway Pumpkin* (Lewis 2003)
Web by LoisAnn Arnold
   In this web, note that the teachers added extension activities to several interest areas after seeing how much the children enjoyed what they had planned.

## Creative Arts

- Make pumpkin prints by dipping little pumpkins in paint and using them to decorate paper.

- Add pumpkin pie spice to orange playdough. Use pumpkin-shaped cookie cutters or mold into pumpkins.

- Mix red and yellow paint together to make the color orange.

- Collect pumpkin seeds and glue them to paper.

## Language Arts

- Create felt board stories related to the story (for example, "Five Little Pumpkins").

- Read other pumpkin books.

- Make pumpkin puppets out of orange socks.

- Imitate and guess farm animal sounds.

## Science

- Open up a pumpkin in the sensory table and explore the goop inside.

- Collect pumpkin vines.

- Collect different kinds of seeds, including pumpkin, and plant them in pots of soil or in wet paper towels inside plastic sandwich bags. What happens?

# Toddler Book Web

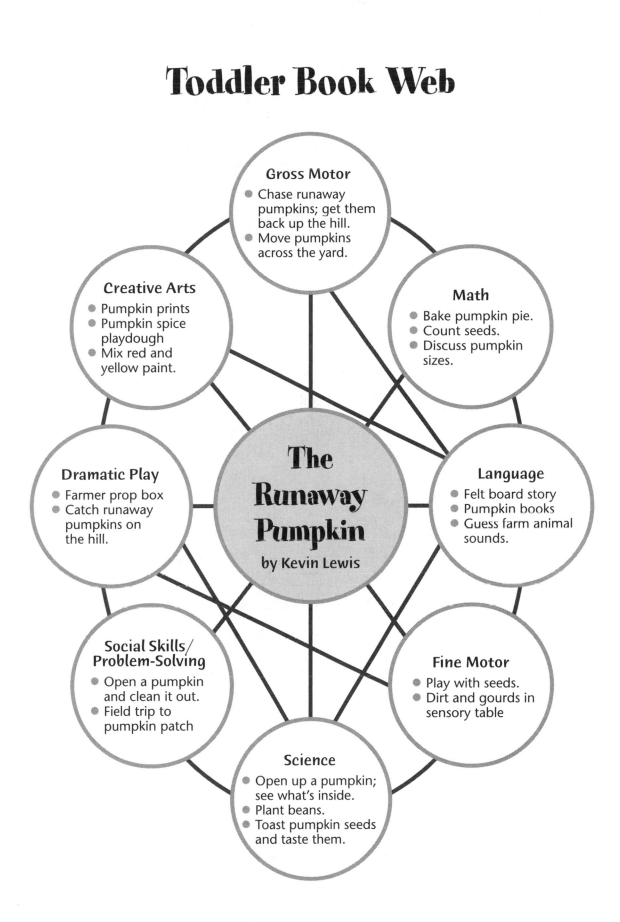

**Gross Motor**
- Chase runaway pumpkins; get them back up the hill.
- Move pumpkins across the yard.

**Creative Arts**
- Pumpkin prints
- Pumpkin spice playdough
- Mix red and yellow paint.

**Math**
- Bake pumpkin pie.
- Count seeds.
- Discuss pumpkin sizes.

**Dramatic Play**
- Farmer prop box
- Catch runaway pumpkins on the hill.

**The Runaway Pumpkin**
by Kevin Lewis

**Language**
- Felt board story
- Pumpkin books
- Guess farm animal sounds.

**Social Skills/Problem-Solving**
- Open a pumpkin and clean it out.
- Field trip to pumpkin patch

**Fine Motor**
- Play with seeds.
- Dirt and gourds in sensory table

**Science**
- Open up a pumpkin; see what's inside.
- Plant beans.
- Toast pumpkin seeds and taste them.

## Fine Motor

- Put dirt in the sensory table with rakes and little gourds: kids make holes for them the way the farmer did.

- Put water in the sensory table with floating pumpkin seeds.

- Explore textures of the pumpkin: the outside, the inside, and the stem.

## Math

- Bake pumpkin bread, pumpkin soup, pumpkin pie.

- Describe pumpkin sizes: large, medium, small.

- Sort and count seeds.

- Play matching games with farm animals and pumpkins.

## Social Studies

- Field trip to Rogers' Produce; pick pumpkins from the pumpkin patch; go on a hay ride pulled by a tractor; pet or meet several farm animals.

- Talk about farms and farmers.

- Have a feast day: bring in food to share at lunch.

## Dramatic Play

- Hide pumpkins around the room or outside, and look for them.

- Dress up like farmers.

- Play with farm animals and a barn.

## Gross Motor

- Chase pumpkins down the hill.

- Roll pumpkins back up the hill.

- Move pumpkins around the playground.

# Preschooler Book Web

*How Do Dinosaurs Say Good Night?* (Yolen 2000)
Web by Megan VanDerZee

As children's language and turn-taking skills develop, they enjoy participating in the planning process. The children in this group were particularly excited by dramatic play and art activities, so creative and dramatic elements spilled over into all the interest areas. Note that activities for older children can involve more steps and self-direction; these teachers stayed close to facilitate problem solving and echo children's observations while they were role-playing dinosaurs, for example.

## Creative Arts

- Make dinosaur masks using paper plates, and decorate them.

- Make dinosaur hand puppets, and act out the story.

- Use instruments to make dinosaur sounds.

- Create a story about dinosaurs doing other things (how do dinosaurs eat dinner?).

## Fine Motor

- Mold dinosaurs out of playdough or clay.

- Create dinosaur prints using paint and construction paper.

- Make a picture and letter collage (for the letters H, D, S, and G) using magazines.

# Preschooler Book Web

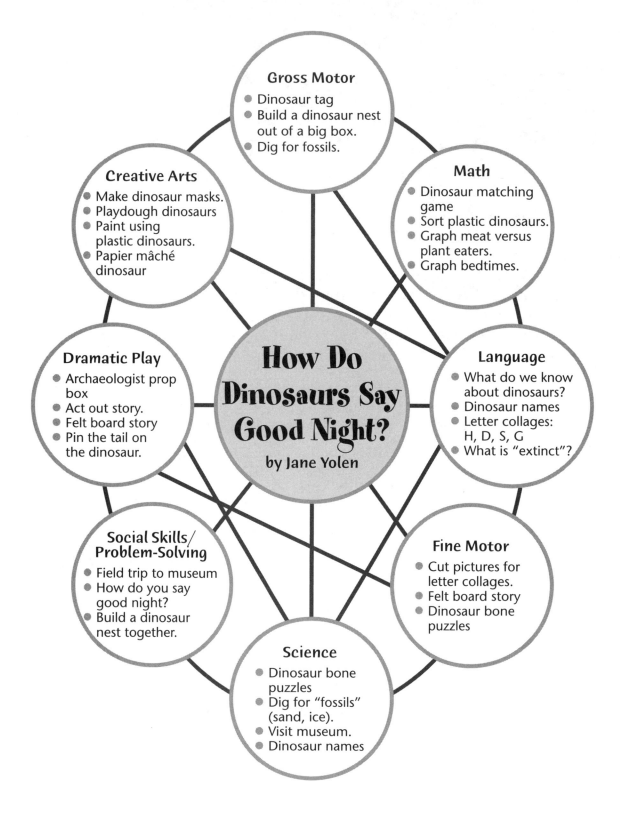

**Gross Motor**
- Dinosaur tag
- Build a dinosaur nest out of a big box.
- Dig for fossils.

**Creative Arts**
- Make dinosaur masks.
- Playdough dinosaurs
- Paint using plastic dinosaurs.
- Papier mâché dinosaur

**Math**
- Dinosaur matching game
- Sort plastic dinosaurs.
- Graph meat versus plant eaters.
- Graph bedtimes.

**Dramatic Play**
- Archaeologist prop box
- Act out story.
- Felt board story
- Pin the tail on the dinosaur.

**How Do Dinosaurs Say Good Night?**
by Jane Yolen

**Language**
- What do we know about dinosaurs?
- Dinosaur names
- Letter collages: H, D, S, G
- What is "extinct"?

**Social Skills/Problem-Solving**
- Field trip to museum
- How do you say good night?
- Build a dinosaur nest together.

**Fine Motor**
- Cut pictures for letter collages.
- Felt board story
- Dinosaur bone puzzles

**Science**
- Dinosaur bone puzzles
- Dig for "fossils" (sand, ice).
- Visit museum.
- Dinosaur names

## Dramatic Play

- Act out the story, allowing each child to be a dinosaur.

## Gross Motor

- Decorate a large box as a dinosaur nest.
- Move around the gym like a dinosaur.

## Language Arts

- Make felt board pieces (Dad, Mom, dinosaurs, bedroom items) for the kids to tell the story in their own words.
- Ask what some of the differences are between people and dinosaurs.
- Ask what the world would be like if dinosaurs were alive today (cause and effect).
- Talk about the meaning of "extinct." Talk about how children think dinosaurs became extinct.
- Talk about what children's rooms look like at home.
- Talk about the different moms and dads the dinosaurs have in the story.
- Ask how the dinosaurs' families are similar to or different from their own.
- Ask children to share their bedtime routine at home. How do they say good night?
- Have children create their own book, "How do children say good night?"
- Ask which other animals are similar to dinosaurs.
- Read other dinosaur books.

## Science

- Have rocks, sand, and dinosaurs in the sensory table.

- Grow "dinosaur food."

- Classify dinosaurs by what they eat.

- Freeze plastic dinosaurs and have children pick at the ice like a paleontologist.

- Go on a fossil hunt outside using magnifying glasses, small brushes, and shovels.

- Collect items outside that dinosaurs might have eaten, used, had around, etc., when they were alive.

## Math

- Make a matching game with dinosaur pictures from the story and their names.

- Sort colored dinosaurs.

- Count how many different dinosaurs are in the story.

- Graph which dinosaurs from the story are meat eaters versus plant eaters.

- Graph what time each child goes to bed at night.

## Social Studies

- Take a trip to a museum to see a dinosaur exhibit.

- Have a dinosaur hunt: hide plastic dinosaurs around the room, and have everyone hunt.

- Play pin the tail on the dinosaur.

## Answers to the Question "What Do We Know about Dinosaurs?"

Ellen: That they eat lots of things but are not alive because they are extinct. They also aren't allowed in preschool, but wouldn't it be silly if they were allowed in preschool?

Ethan: That the Allosaurus stuffs his body with meat, because I heard that from the poem of Allosaurus. And if dinosaurs and people were alive, the meat eaters would eat us. But they wouldn't like our wax or hair. I also know a fossil is a footprint left in the mud of a dinosaur pond when the dinosaur died.

Hannah: That the hugest dinosaur of all is the Allosaurus.

Peter: That they eat lots of stuff like meat.

John: Some eat flowers.

Lucas: I know about hundreds and hundreds of dinosaur bones.

# Older Preschooler and Kindergartner Book Web

*Sylvester and the Magic Pebble* (Steig 1969)
   Older preschoolers and kindergarteners are fairly concrete: they love to gather evidence and collect objects. This interest is reflected in the many cause-and-effect activities the group planned for this web, including hide-and-seek, making packing lists, and brainstorming safety suggestions. As with the other age groups, this web changed slightly between the graphic and text versions. For example, hiding and finding a "magic pebble" was not a satisfying task for a large group, even though it was directly related to the book. These concrete thinkers thought there should be only one pebble (as in the book), and most of the kids began feeling too competitive to enjoy the game. Instead, the teachers set up a hide-and-seek game in which it was acceptable (to the kids) to have many objects to find. Although there was no category for music on the graphic web, teachers found several complementary listening activities and added them during the course of the project. Language arts activities grow increasingly complex as children prepare to read; note that the selected activities cover a range of pre-reading skills: speaking, listening, phonemic awareness, and rehearsal. This provides interest for kids at varying stages of reading development.

# Older Preschooler and Kindergartner Book Web

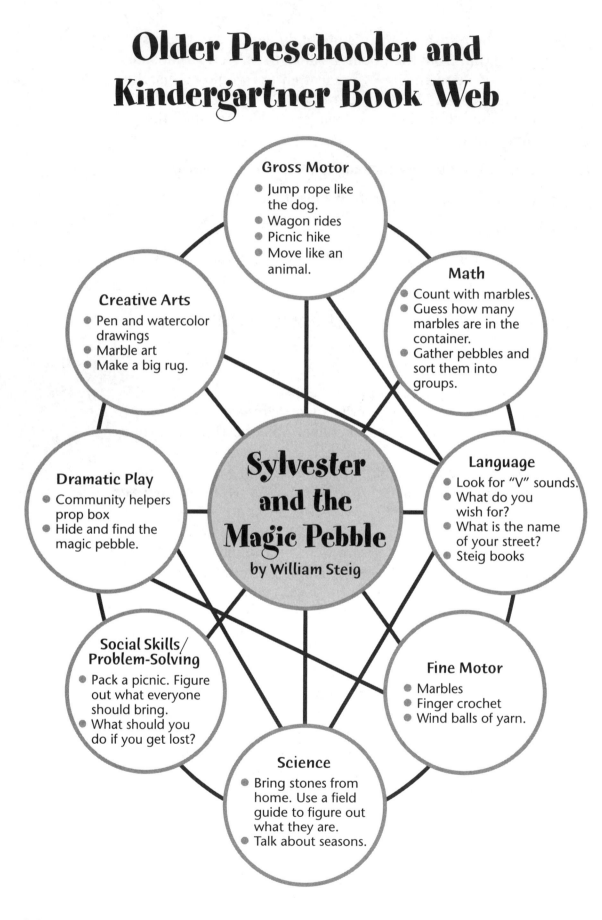

**Gross Motor**
- Jump rope like the dog.
- Wagon rides
- Picnic hike
- Move like an animal.

**Math**
- Count with marbles.
- Guess how many marbles are in the container.
- Gather pebbles and sort them into groups.

**Creative Arts**
- Pen and watercolor drawings
- Marble art
- Make a big rug.

**Language**
- Look for "V" sounds.
- What do you wish for?
- What is the name of your street?
- Steig books

**Dramatic Play**
- Community helpers prop box
- Hide and find the magic pebble.

## Sylvester and the Magic Pebble
### by William Steig

**Fine Motor**
- Marbles
- Finger crochet
- Wind balls of yarn.

**Social Skills/ Problem-Solving**
- Pack a picnic. Figure out what everyone should bring.
- What should you do if you get lost?

**Science**
- Bring stones from home. Use a field guide to figure out what they are.
- Talk about seasons.

## Art

- Use black pens to draw pictures and watercolor to color them.

- Marble art: roll marbles in paint and across paper in a tray.

- Fold a paper in four sections. Draw the same scene in four seasons on the same page.

- Do finger crochet with yarn.

- Make your own patterns on shirt and dress outlines.

## Math

- Count marbles. Use marbles to count how many years old the whole class is.

- Guess how many marbles are in a jar. Use a circle of string and fill it with marbles. Count them and estimate how many layers of marbles will fill the jar.

- Gather pebbles from the neighborhood. Sort them different ways: size, color, texture (smooth or rough).

- Count the dogs in the book. Graph the kinds and numbers of pets children have at home.

- Learn the name for the shape of a marble ("sphere"). Find other spheres in the class and outside: balls, peas, the globe, eggs ("they are smooshed spheres"), oranges, apples, pom-poms, beads, ball of yarn. Ian said, "*Spheres* is very hard to spell."

- What are the patterns in this book?

## Science

- Bring stones from home. Use a rock and mineral guide to figure out what the names are for everyone's rocks. Talk about the three types of rocks (sedimentary, igneous, and metamorphic) and how they are made.

- Talk about the seasons in Michigan. Figure out who else has weather like ours. Pick a place on the map (Mississippi), and figure out what their seasons look like.

- Chart the weather. Guess which months have rain, thunder, and lightning.

- Look for flower buds. Draw them.

## Music

- Listen to the "summer storms" CD.

- Try to howl like a wolf. Listen to a tape of wolves howling that someone's parents found.

- Try to sound like a donkey and the other animals in the book.

## Social Skills and Problem-Solving

- Pack a picnic. Figure out what we need for lunch. Have everybody bring something.

- Who are helpers in our community?

- Hide a "pebble" (small red ball), and play "Hot and Cold" to find it.

- Talk about getting lost. Make a list of things you can do when you get lost.

Things You Can Do If You Get Lost

- Look for a helper.

- Yell for your mom and dad.

- Stay where you are so someone can find you.

- Look for another mommy and ask her for help.

Things You Can Do So You Don't Get Lost

- Hold somebody's hand.

- Use a walkie-talkie.

- Stay where you can see your mom and dad.

- Use the buddy system.

- Wear a bell.

- Learn your mom and dad's (cell) phone numbers so a helper can call them.

- Don't run away.

- Use a map.

## Language Arts

- Look for things that have a "vuh" sound in their name.

- What do you wish for? Make a poster.

- What is the name of your street? Practice writing your address.

- Tape-record several parents reading the book in a continuous loop.

- Look on the bookshelves to find other books by William Steig. How are they the same? How are they different?

## Fine Motor

- Play marbles.

- Learn how to finger crochet.

- Wind and unwind balls of yarn.

## Gross Motor

- Try to jump rope like the dog.

- Give each other wagon rides.

- Hike to the park for a picnic.

## Dramatic Play

- Make a community helpers prop box.

- Move like a donkey, wolf, pig, chicken, lion. Have everyone guess what you are.

- Play doggy hide-and-seek, and look for hidden "bones" (crackers).

# Looking Ahead

Although this book is designed to show teachers how to weave their own book-based webs, experimenting with the completed webs in this chapter may help you sell the process to staff who are unsure about it. Remember that even though those webs worked well for their groups, they might not be as successful for a different group of children. The real key to weaving an engaging book web is starting with an appropriate book. Chapter 5 explains tools and techniques for observing children's behavior to choose books that reflect their developmental needs and interests.

# References

Carle, Eric. 1969. *The very hungry caterpillar.* New York: Philomel.

Lewis, Kevin. 2003. *The runaway pumpkin.* New York: Orchard.

Steig, William. 1969. *Sylvester and the magic pebble.* New York: Windmill.

Yolen, Jane. 2000. *How do dinosaurs say good night?* New York: Blue Sky.

# 5

# Observing Children's Interests

When I was a toddler teacher, I had a group of four boisterous boys who went through a phase in which they were obsessed with bodily functions. They loved to talk about body parts and going to the bathroom. They peppered their speech with "poopy" this, "poopy" that. At home, one child helped his parents clean up after their dog, and then brought that activity to the playground. He showed the other kids how to use snow shovels to gather piles of twigs and move them around the yard. When we went for a neighborhood walk and passed a yard with two dogs, which apparently hadn't been cleaned for months, the boys were speechless—not disgusted, but impressed. Coincidentally, a friend of mine gave me a book called *Everyone Poops* by Taro Gomi. It's a matter-of-fact explanation that uses frank language, simple art, and a humorous tone. Since one of the standard suggestions to reduce potty talk is to remain matter-of-fact about it, I thought this book would be perfect for story time. I couldn't wait to share it. But when I read it to the kids, it went over like a lead balloon. They weren't amused or entertained. I was perplexed until I took a couple of giant steps back and realized that this wasn't about poop at all. These boys were two-and-a-half and three years old. They liked to test limits and were just realizing the power of language—their poop talk was all about getting a reaction. Talking nonstop about going to the bathroom was also part of their very recent mastery of the process: recognizing the need to go to the bathroom and rehearsing all the steps associated with being successful. The yard cleanup was related to increasing independence and responsibility. And their awe at the messy lawn? I think they were impressed with the sheer number of piles. They could have been piles of twigs or apples or tennis balls and gotten the same reaction. It was simply a lot of stuff to look at. In this case, I wasn't paying close enough attention to their individual interests (autonomy, language, counting), and I didn't consider the developmental context of their behavior. Thinking about those things would have helped me find more relevant books and helped me build on their inspired imaginative play, instead of merely being amused by it.

When you plan your first book-based curriculum web, it will be tempting to pick one of your own favorite books because you already know their themes inside and out. You might even have preplanned units ready to go. Why not start with those and ease into the child-chosen books? Because book-based webbing is supposed to be about children's interests and discoveries, not only yours. It's a journey teachers and children take together.

You might also want to use books that you know your children will enjoy or that you believe have the broadest potential. Resist the temptation to choose "easy" books; they'll only lead to uninspired webs. Ongoing observation will help you discern the topics children find intriguing and figure out complementary books and activities to enrich your classroom. Before you even begin selecting books to web, you must take time to stop, look, and listen.

# Observing Children's Interests: Stop!

If you ask a young child what he likes about a book, his answers are likely to be superficial: the cover, the fact that his friend wanted it, or the fact that he's seen it on a bookshelf elsewhere. But if you watch a young child shop for books or retell stories, you'll learn a lot about what makes her tick. Considering children's book choices in a variety of settings is the best way to understand their interests. Use these questions to ensure you're taking a wide-angle view of book use in your classroom.

## Do the Books in Your Classroom Cover a Wide Range of Topics?

Most teachers rotate the books they put out according to curricular themes and available space. Reading a variety of books on a single subject will enhance children's understanding of that topic, but teachers should also provide books on a variety of subjects at all times. Even infants and toddlers need a variety in their literary diet. For example, books can provide very young children the safe distance they need to study things like animals that may be scary in real life. All children make sense of the world by drawing connections between the things they see and experience. If we encourage their natural tendency to think divergently, they'll often draw interesting connections between things adults perceive as unrelated. Children also need opportunities and invitations to branch out to other interests. So a well-balanced, thoughtfully selected classroom library is a prerequisite for having a truly child-directed, book-based curriculum.

## Do the Children in Your Class Have an Opportunity to Choose Books for the Group?

In many programs, teachers select the books to read aloud at circle time. This is a great way to introduce new titles and reinforce themes and concepts, but it shouldn't replace child-selected read-alouds. Choosing a book or two for circle time is a great classroom job for a preschooler or kindergartner. Encouraging children to share books from home will increase the number and variety of books the students experience; it also makes story time more child-centered. Class trips to the library will further broaden children's horizons.

## Do the Children in Your Class Have Time to Read Alone?

Teachers should read aloud to children every day. Hopefully, this won't happen only in a large-group setting. Children should also have opportunities to read alone throughout the day. Making books a fixture in the classroom and including them in interest centers will help, but you may also want to schedule a silent reading session. Before nap (or after lunch for older classes) is the perfect time to give children a chance to really pore over books, and the quiet setting makes it convenient for teachers to take note of their choices. Once your classroom library is in good shape and you are providing a variety of reading experiences, it's time to start taking notes.

# Observing Children's Interests: Look!

Observing young children at play presents dual challenges: finding the time to observe and recording observations in a meaningful and useful manner. Whether your observations are casual classroom notes or formal assessment checklists, paying attention to your students' interests, struggles, and thrills will help you weave a more engaging and developmentally appropriate curriculum web.

## On-the-Spot Observation

Even new teachers and teachers in a transitional program can manage simple observations with a bit of forethought. The most basic kind of classroom observation is informal, on-the-spot mental note-taking. At the beginning of the day, give yourself and your co-teachers an assignment, or watchword. "Today, let's watch for _____." Some examples are popular toys, sources of conflict, popular interest centers, books children choose, who plays together, themes in imaginative play. The watchword you choose will depend on your group's needs and your teaching goals. Subsequent watchwords will become more specific and/or sophisticated as you incorporate changes and new ideas based on earlier observations.

## Comparing Notes

If your children nap, use that opportunity to take ten to fifteen minutes to share your observations with other staff and incorporate them into your immediate and long-term plans. If you notice, for example, that the children were reluctant to finish a particular activity, you might rearrange your afternoon to give them more time to explore it.

If your children don't nap or if naptime is used for breaks and meetings, a classroom notebook can help. At the top of each page, record the date and the item you're watching for. Teachers can add notes when they have a free moment, and other teachers can add questions or suggestions as they come up. This record is also useful at room meetings: teachers can examine a long-term record of the classroom dynamics and children's interests and needs.

# Building a Better Note-Trap

Mental note-taking can happen every day without interrupting the program or requiring additional staff, but there's always the chance that your insights won't actually make it into your staff conversations or notebook. Teaching duties may also interfere with the level of attention you are able to pay to individual and group observations. It's impossible to be 100 percent reporter and 100 percent teacher at the same time, and dividing your efforts may diminish the success of either aspect of the job.

You can increase the detail and accuracy of on-the-fly observations by using an observation form (or index cards) with blanks determined by the information you're trying to glean. For example, if you have a child who's biting in a toddler group or a kindergartner with aggressive tendencies, you would include the following items for each incident: name, date, issue, who was involved, source of conflict, resolution.

This kind of note-taking can help you discover patterns of behavior and work toward reducing contributing factors. The example above concerns behavioral issues, but this information will help you plan curriculum that recognizes children's social skills, problem-solving, and group dynamics.

# Older Toddler Observation Form

Name: _Tomas_

Date: _October 16, 2003_

Issue: _Melanie refused to share trains with any other kids. Tomas pushed Melanie and took them._

Who else was involved: _Tomas, Melanie, Aiden_

Source of conflict: _Not enough trains? Not enough other activities? Tomas has trouble waiting._

Resolution: _Asked kids if they want to divide them up or take turns with all of them. Used timer to keep track. Gave Tomas a train book while he waited._

# Formalities

Using checklists or making your own will help you focus your casual observations, but stepping out of the teacher role to simply sit and observe helps teachers note specific details about individual needs and interests. It also provides information about staff-student interactions.

Formal observation time can be free-form or focused with individual and group checklists. Using both kinds of note-taking will provide a more balanced view of a program's successes and challenges. Teachers' personal interests shape their individual observations to bring balance to the classroom and lead to new insights, so try to give all the staff who work in your room a chance to observe. If you know that a particular staff member (or child!) is especially good with a particular aspect of curriculum, assign observations accordingly.

Scheduling time to observe can be challenging. When you change the adults who are actually working with the kids by taking one out to observe, the group dynamics will change. It's important to relieve the observing teacher with someone whom the children know and with whom they're comfortable. Teachers in nearby classrooms, long-term or regular substitutes, paraprofessionals, parent volunteers, and supervisory staff may all fit this bill.

In many early childhood programs, there are points in the day when teachers take turns being in charge. Although it might seem convenient to observe while one teacher does story time or another large-group activity, this probably isn't the best way to study students' interests and abilities. The children will be focused on the teacher, and they'll be part of a much larger student-to-teacher ratio. In a toddler classroom, going from a 1:4 to a 1:8 ratio (or in a preschool group, from 1:9 to 1:18) will have a significant impact on children's behavior, even if it's only for a short period of time. Consider hiring a familiar substitute who can spend one hour each in several different classrooms on the same day. Ideally, you could do this at least once a month (or more, depending on the size of your center) to develop a familiar routine for children and staff and to ensure that the observations happen consistently.

When you've established staff coverage for formal observation time, be sure to vary the times of day and group sizes that you study. Children's and teachers' energy levels rise and fall throughout the day. Consider these natural rhythms during your observations and later planning to help you plan activities that match children's needs for quiet and active play.

# Observing Children's Interests: Listen!

Remember to ask for parent feedback about students' interests and abilities. The first time to ask for this kind of information is at enrollment or at the start of each school year. Part of the child information questionnaire should include the question "What kinds of books does your child love to read?" Gathering this information at transition time is especially helpful because books are a nonthreatening, universally engaging way to help a new child feel comfortable and to help a group of children identify and relate to common interests.

Establishing routines for sharing books from home makes families feel welcome and emphasizes the importance of books in children's lives. Consider ideas like these:

- "Bring a Book from Home Day"

- incorporating favorite books into star of the week, birthday celebrations, and other special rituals

- inviting parents to be guest readers once a week or once a month

- gathering book bags that include a book, related objects, and a simple activity for children to share with their families on a rotating basis

Staff should also invite parents to provide favorite-book feedback throughout the year. Teachers can post lists with headings such as "What we're reading at home" on a bulletin board or clipboard. Parents from other countries can help broaden your classroom library by sharing or donating books representing their culture that aren't available for purchase in the United States.

Once you've gathered input from staff and parents, use your notes to make book lists to take to the library, bookstore, and activity-planning meetings. Post them so parents can make suggestions or share related books from home. Identifying recurring themes and developmental issues will help you select books (and activities) that challenge, delight, and inspire the children in your classroom. Once you know what makes the children in your class tick, you can build your classroom library around their interests. Chapter 6 will help you evaluate texts, find funds for new books, repurpose old books, and organize your library into a useful and manageable system.

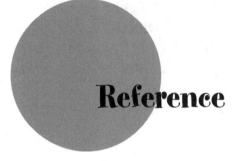

# Reference

Gomi, Taro. 1993. *Everyone poops.* Brooklyn, N.Y.: Kane/Miller.

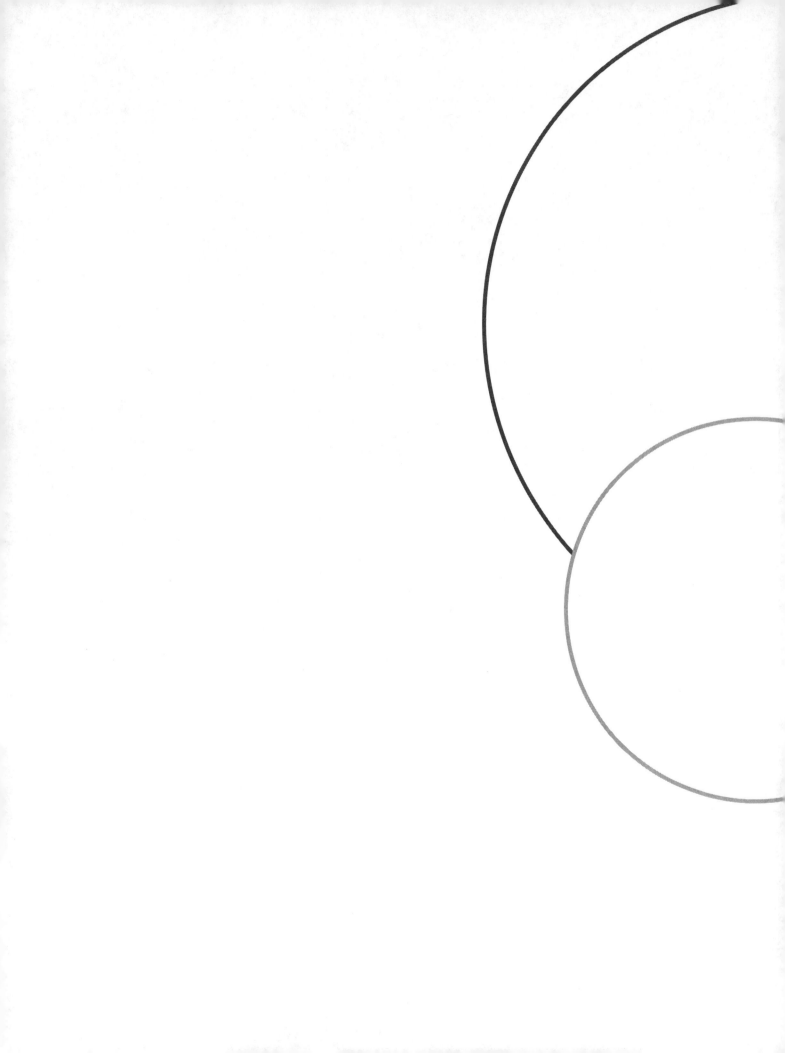

# 6 Building a Classroom Library

Some adults argue that any book is a good book if it gets kids interested in reading and keeps them hooked, but this approach is simplistic. A bag of potato chips is better than no food at all, but it's not a nutritious snack, and few would call it a meal—or recommend eating potato chips three times a day. Many adults believe, however, that a book that is little more than a commercial for a television character or toy is a fine thing for a child to read. It's true that even "junky" books have letters to decode, vocabulary words to acquire, and plots to follow. If a commercial book attracts a TV-obsessed child who otherwise wouldn't pick up a book, at least it's a start. But overall, I consider these books to be like junk food: fine for an occasional snack, but a poor substitute for long-term brain food.

Extremely boring writing can be a turnoff. Text and art that depict cultural stereotypes can damage a non-majority child's self-esteem and instill or enforce biases in others. Some junky books are factually incorrect. There is so much high-quality literature available for young children that child care centers and preschool programs need not stock their literary pantries with potato chips and Twinkies.

A curriculum web is only as strong as the book it's spun around. Many people know a good book when they read one, but don't know what made it a good book or how to find another good one. This chapter will help you with these tasks:

- evaluate books for content and presentation

- collect books that cover a broad range of topics as well as explore subjects in depth

- use creative resources to buy, borrow, and re-use books

- display and use books in ways that give children choices about what they read while protecting this precious resource

- store and sort books in ways that help teachers make the most use of them

# Nutritious Books

Although taste in literature is subjective, quality books have concrete characteristics that teachers can look for. Developmental needs determine appropriate content for different age groups, but, in general, good books share several traits. Substantial stories have interesting, multidimensional characters, a compelling plot, and rich language.

## Characters

What makes characters interesting? Imperfection. Characters who do everything right are boring. Children of all ages are constantly working to master new skills, so they identify with characters who struggle and make mistakes. They're particularly interested in seeing how characters handle their mistakes: how they fix things, how they manage their emotions, whether they change their behavior as a result. A character who faces no obstacles won't sustain a reader's interest for very long.

Unusual people are also very intriguing. Children reading stories about people unlike themselves are fascinated by those characters' differences from *and* similarities to their own experience. Quality multicultural literature can give children insight into other cultures or reflect the beauty of their own cultural traditions. "Multicultural" is a term most often applied to literature about people of color, but truly multicultural books address more than skin color. They portray people of varying socioeconomic status. They also show nontraditional families—single parents, grandparents as caregivers, parents with disabilities, and so on. And true anti-bias literature includes characters who don't behave according to typical gender- and culture-stereotyped roles (fathers who are bread-winning disciplinarians, mothers who are nurturing caregivers). This is to suggest not that the "classic" nuclear family has no place in classroom books, but that other ways of life should be represented. The images and words in children's literature form lasting impressions for young children—impressions about society's expectations for them and for the people they'll meet throughout life. Classroom libraries must reflect children's daily lives *as well as* introduce them to other possibilities.

Some teachers adopt a tourist approach to multiculturalism and purchase books that focus on holidays or special events; they may only showcase these books in association with a particular unit or time of year. A culturally relevant library features families from many cultures engaged in the everyday aspects of family life and illuminates their unique celebrations and traditions. As you browse through books, ask yourself: Are the characters and settings (as portrayed in the text and the art) culturally authentic? Do they include realistic details and accurate information?

Sometimes interesting characters are not imperfect—in fact, they've got superhuman skills! They are exciting to read about because children vicariously experience all that power. The exaggeration of personal characteristics (positive and negative) is also intriguing. A diverse library should include some books about idealized situations involving "superkids" or folktale legends.

# Plot

A compelling plot includes a problem: a main character who wants something desperately or who has an obstacle to overcome. Struggle is stimulating, and conflict is captivating—it's human nature. The conflict does not have to be serious or dangerous—for a toddler, an interesting conflict could involve something as simple as sharing toys or moving to a big-kid bed. For older children who are more peer-focused, conflict often involves personality issues or fears such as being alone, getting lost, or losing a beloved toy. But in order for readers to care about a character, we must know what makes him tick.

As you consider plot, beware of pedantic, preachy books. A great story will have meaningful themes woven into the plot without hitting the reader over the head with them. Children can spot a lesson coming a mile a way, and they are likely to tune it out if it's heavy-handed. Drawing their own conclusions after reading a story helps children feel powerful and internalize positive messages. Circle time conversations will further help children clarify and digest themes and outcomes.

# Language

Quality children's books have rich language beginning with the adjectives and verbs the writer uses to tell his or her story. Some words are so overused in everyday talk that they become almost meaningless—"nice," "good," "bad," and "fun" are just a few examples. They're not descriptive, they don't have interesting sounds that attract young listeners, and they don't move the story forward. Some adults say that these words are simple and that simple things are good for young minds. But this doesn't take into account children's remarkable receptive vocabularies, the words they recognize and understand. Even very young children can understand many more words than they can pronounce or recall and use correctly in a sentence. When children are exposed to new words, they first learn to recognize and understand them, and then later begin to use them in their own speech. Exposure to a varied vocabulary from an early age helps children tune into new sounds and words and incorporate them into their own expressive vocabulary, the words they use in everyday speech. Good books will use context to explain the meaning of unfamiliar words. Reading these kinds of stories regularly also improves children's comprehension skills because listening for contextual clues becomes a habit.

Poetic and playful language isn't merely fun. It enhances children's phonemic awareness: recognition of the discrete sounds that make up the syllables of language. Being able to discriminate between similar sounds is a key skill for reading and writing success. The format that the author uses to tell the story can also encourage children to participate, as in call-and-response books or books that incorporate sounds and gestures. The more senses a child uses as she reads, the more meaning the story takes on for her.

Here are some of the devices that writers use to enhance language:

- *Alliteration,* which uses words that begin with the same sounds: *The four fat foxes flung their fish as far as they could.*

- *Assonance,* a kind of internal rhyme in which words share the same vowel sounds, but not consonants: *The shaking made the cake fall off the plate.*

- *Consonance,* which uses words that share consonant sounds, but not vowels: *Betty bought a bit of bitter butter for her batter.*

- *Onomatopoeia,* or words that sound just like what they describe: *Boom! Splash! Kerplop!*

Rhyme builds phonemic awareness and helps children predict what will happen next. Pre-readers can be active participants in story time, and beginning readers can use rhyming patterns to help them decode spelling. But just because a story rhymes doesn't make it good. Numerous near-rhymes (such as "again" and "friend" or "again" and "rain") in a single story can be confusing. The meter of a rhyming story is also critical: each line must have the right number of stressed and unstressed syllables. You don't need to take a poetry course to recognize good meter, however. If the reader must hurry to fit everything in or stretch words out to make them fit, the rhyme probably isn't very good.

## Don't Forget the Pictures!

When choosing picture books, adults must consider art as carefully as they consider text. Consider these criteria as you evaluate picture-book art:

- Is the book beautiful and appealing? There is simply too much beautiful art available to waste time and money on mediocre books.

- Does the art tell a story without the words? This makes a book more versatile since children can pore over and contemplate it during quiet moments alone.

- Is the art thoughtful? Thoughtful illustrations add layers to the story that the text cannot or does not reveal. Some stories have entire secondary story lines in the art. This engages readers who are more visual than auditory, and makes a book interesting for subsequent readings and for a wide range of ages.

- Does the art illuminate the story? Art shouldn't merely illustrate the exact words, but fill in any blanks and shed light on the characters.

- Is the art developmentally appropriate? Art should also grow more technically complex with more mature books because older children can process more intricate images and finer lines.

## Does the Book Make Sense?

The last criterion for evaluating books is the most basic: art, text, concepts, and language should be developmentally appropriate. A book that is perfect for an older preschooler may not be appropriate for younger children. But just because a book is written for toddlers does not mean that older children can't enjoy it. Rather than be limited by publisher-determined age ranges, teachers can ask themselves a few questions before selecting or rejecting a book for classroom use:

- Do the characters and situations in this story relate to my children's experiences?

- With younger children, is the text simple enough to hold their attention? If not, consider shortening the text as you read aloud or putting lengthy passages into your own words if the art is appropriate.

- With older children, is the text complex enough to hold their attention? If not, consider the book's value as a springboard to other books and activities on the subject. It might also be appropriate for an early-reader shelf in an older preschool or a kindergarten classroom.

# Evaluating Books: An Exercise

Using the checklist below, evaluate a representative sample of books from your own classroom. Assign the books numbers, and record your observations for each. Have other teachers evaluate the same books; then compare your results. Consult resources such as *Start Seeing Diversity* (Wolpert 1999), *Through Indian Eyes* (Slapin & Seale 1998), *Black Books Galore!* (Rand, Parker, and Foster 1998), and *Lessons from Turtle Island* (Jones & Moomaw 2002) to help you assess books for stereotypes and bias. The Council on Inter-racial Books for Children produced several checklists on the topic of bias in children's books, which can still be found in some of the above books and other resources, even though CIBC itself is no longer active. Consider these questions: What are some of the strengths of your collection? What are some of its weaknesses? Then make a list of things to look for as you search for new books for your classroom. Share this list with anyone who buys books for your room, including administrators, other teachers, and parents.

## Checklist: Evaluating Books for Classroom Use

### Character

- Do the characters behave like the children in my class?

- Do the characters have flaws?

- Do the characters represent people of color and women in a positive light and as active participants in the story?

- Do the characters perpetuate stereotypes?

### Story

- Does this story have a problem or quest?

- Is the story's problem or quest relevant to my students' age group?

- Do the characters struggle to solve their own problems?

- Is the ending satisfying?

## Language

- Does the text use strong adjectives and verbs?

- Does the text use rich language sounds (for example, alliteration or onomatopoeia)?

- If the story rhymes, does it have a good meter? Does the rhyme enhance the story?

## Art

- Is the art attractive? thoughtful? interesting?

- Does the art merely illustrate the exact text, or does it elevate the story?

- Can a child who doesn't read follow the story in the art?

- Are the settings and people pictured authentically?

## Developmental Appropriateness

- Are the concepts and issues in this story relevant to my class?

- Is the sentence length and vocabulary appropriate? Can difficult words be understood with context?

- Is the story length appropriate for my students' age group?

## Authenticity

- Is the story factually correct?

- If it's a fantasy (talking animals, etc.), is it believable?

- If the book is nonfiction, is the explanation clear and understandable for my group?

- If the book is nonfiction, is the subject approached in a creative and lively manner?

## Bottom Line

- Is this a book I would want to read more than once?

- Is there another book that handles this subject in a more accessible or engaging manner?

# Building a Library, Book by Book

Many classrooms reflect teachers' individual interests and taste: they are strong on one kind of book and weak on others. One way to ensure that a book collection is diverse is to have several adults select books for the collection. Just like grown-ups, children's tastes vary, and one child's delight may leave another yawning. Most children's books fall into a few basic categories:

- Slice-of-life stories, which focus on the rituals and pleasures of everyday life. For example: *Goodnight Moon* (Wise 1947)

- Bad-behavior books, which are self-explanatory. For example: *No, David!* (Shannon 1998), *Where the Wild Things Are* (Sendak 1964)

- Relationship books, which celebrate special people in a child's life. For example: *Guess How Much I Love You* (McBratney 1995)

- Adventure books. For example: *The Little Mouse, the Red Ripe Strawberry, and the Big Hungry Bear* (Wood 1990)

- Poetry. For example: *Mother Goose, A Child's Garden of Verses* (Stevenson 1999), *When We Were Very Young* (Milne 1926)

- Party books, which are often musical and are fun, rhythmic celebrations of language and/or everyday events. For example: *Chicka Chicka Boom Boom* (Martin and Archambault 1989)

- Nonfiction books, which are designed primarily to teach. For example: *What Do You Do with a Tail Like This?* (Page 2003)

- Concept books, such as alphabet books, books about colors, etc. For example: *It Looked Like Spilt Milk* (Shaw 1947)

- Issue books, which cover subjects such as death, self-esteem, separation anxiety, etc. For example: *William's Doll* (Zolotow 1972)

- Folktales. For example: *Tikki Tikki Tembo* (Mosel 1968)

Some books will fit under several of these umbrellas. Another way to sort a collection of books is by the structure of the story itself: talking-animal books, rhyming books, humorous books, call-and-response books, etc. A strong library covers a wide range of subjects, but also explores individual topics in depth. Knowing the strengths and weaknesses of your collection will help you add appropriate titles. When your book budget is limited, try not to duplicate subjects. Having several books that explain different kinds of neighborhoods will give your collection depth, but having several books about the same kinds of transportation doesn't. Instead of buying more books about things with wheels, think about locomotion globally, and think about species other than humans: How do we get from here to there?

# Book Budgets

Many early childhood programs budget costs into two categories: consumable versus permanent. I encourage teachers to consider books consumable (though not disposable!) because if books are used on a daily basis, they will wear out over time. Setting aside money in the budget for good books, then, is the first way to start building your library. If your budget is very lean, consider making a special fund for book buying. This can be a parent-facilitated effort or an ongoing fund. Dedicated bake sales, car washes, and other events are great ways to gather funds for books.

Once you have some money set aside, careful spending will stretch your book-buying dollars even further. Secondhand stores, garage sales, and library sales are great places to buy wonderful, gently used books at a fraction of the cover price. Don't assume that library discards are "bad" books—most librarians have to make room for new books each year. Library discards have the added benefit of reinforced covers and spines.

Book order clubs offer paperback versions of popular titles or significantly discounted hardback editions. Paperbacks are more fragile than hardcovers, of course, but this makes them a lower-risk way to teach young children book-handling behaviors and can let you have several copies of popular titles. If your center participates in book order programs, you'll earn points toward free books for every dollar spent by parents and staff.

Many families like to mark children's milestones (birthdays, transitions to a new classroom, etc.) by donating something to the center. Why not ask them to donate a book? If you keep a wish list of titles and/or types of books you're seeking, you'll make it even easier for them to make a meaningful contribution to the program. Provide bookplates for families to personalize their donations, and publicize new titles in your newsletter as a way to encourage others to participate.

You don't have to pay full price for brand-new titles. Bookstores often have educators' weekends or evenings during which teachers receive hefty discounts off the retail prices for new books. Publishers and book distributors' booths at early childhood and literacy conferences often feature their latest titles at significant discounts. If your community has major corporate employers whose children attend your program, you might consider forming a partnership with them to conduct book drives or other projects.

Don't forget to utilize your local public library to enrich your classroom collection. Librarians will be able to help you find lesser-known books that relate to your activities and themes. Making regular trips to the library will help keep your classroom collection fresh; taking field trips to the library with preschool children will show them how to find information and books on certain topics. Using a list makes shopping for a classroom library more manageable. The end of this chapter has a list of organizations that review and award books; their Web sites can provide book recommendations.

# The Book Hospital

Children who love books will fondle, curl up with, and sometimes taste them as they read. Even gently handled books will eventually fall apart. Clear package tape placed to reinforce the inside page seams will lengthen a book's shelf life; it can also be used to patch small tears and holes. For bigger boo-boos, clear contact paper is a better choice.

Books with pages beyond repair can be repurposed. Cut characters and objects out of the pages and laminate them; then attach magnets or felt to the back for use with storytelling. Laminate or frame any remaining intact pages and use them as classroom art. Hang several in a row to show an abbreviated version of the story, or hang individual illustrations in various interest areas of the room. Post book art in unusual spots—the ceiling, the underside of tables, inside a play loft, on bathroom stalls—to spark children's interest and encourage conversations as they explore the room and play.

# The Care and Feeding of Classroom Books

Space is always at a premium in the early childhood classroom, and safety and conservation issues vary by age group. With all age groups, don't restrict books to a book nook or corner of the classroom. Include relevant titles in all interest areas (books about building or counting in the math area, collage books in the art area, etc.), and encourage children to do the same.

Babies and young toddlers need access to books at their eye level. Milk crates or low shelves keep board books and cloth books within the reach of very young readers. In these class-rooms, teachers should place more fragile books within sight but out of reach, so children can gesture to or ask for a favorite book. Babies will chew, tear, and take apart books as they explore them, so adults should model appropriate book-handling behaviors by reading to the children and giving them chances to touch the books with supervision. The face-out, tiered display shelves popular in early childhood catalogs aren't appropriate for a classroom with crawlers and climbers, whose efforts to scale the shelves will destroy the books and may tip the shelf if it's not bolted to the wall.

Older toddlers and younger preschoolers can understand appropriate treatment of books but will occasionally need reminders. They may throw books when caught up in the excite-ment of the moment or enjoy the physical sensation of tearing paper. Milk crates and low shelves are still good display choices for this age group. Crates or baskets allow children to move books around the classroom as they play, encouraging divergent thinking and cross-discipline connections. Face-out display shelves are appropriate when secured to the wall; books should not be stacked several deep or the children won't be able to find the ones they want without pulling them all out. Another conven-ient perch for books is the top of low shelves, standing with the covers forming a V, pages fanned. Low ledges can provide more face-out space, as can plastic rain gutters attached to the wall as suggested in *The Read-Aloud Handbook* (Trelease 1982).

Preschoolers are able to recognize the spines of favorite books, so some of the books in their classrooms can be shelved spine out. This provides space for the many more titles needed with the greater number of children and higher interest in independent reading of this age group. Dish tubs on top of low shelves let children flip through titles without taking up too much room. With older children, grouping titles by general categories will also help children find the kinds of books they want as well as introduce library concepts. Put a picture and written label on the front of the tub. Ledges, shelf tops, and tier shelves or rotating displays are all good ways to provide face-out space for visually oriented children. Sorting classroom books by various categories is a great activity for older preschoolers and kindergartners. It involves comprehension, observation, and categorization, all important math and reading skills. Some starter categories: animals, people, concepts; first letters of titles; colors; covers. Encourage children to come up with their own criteria for sorting.

# Storing Books

No matter what size your classroom or library, it's probably not possible or advisable to display all your books at once. It's important to store unused books carefully to protect them and keep them accessible. Milk crates can be stacked, so they don't require shelves (books can also make many shelves droop!). If books will be stored in a moist environment like a basement, use plastic crates with lids and put charcoal or newspaper in the box to absorb the mustiness.

Before you store books, use a coding system such as colored circle stickers or colored tape on the spines to help you find subjects quickly. On the outside of the bin or crate, post a key: green = nature, yellow = relationships, etc. Some books will have several appropriate color codes. Rotate titles at least once a month. Library books will never go into storage, but be sure that their location in the classroom will protect them from busy fingers. If you have favorite library books that are out of print and no longer available in stores, keep a list of them in the book folders discussed in Chapter 5.

Whenever you start a web, pull out books that relate directly and tangentially to your web book. Older children will enjoy trying to figure out how they're related and may have suggestions for connections to other books that you haven't even considered. Don't display only books that relate directly to your web, because children will be ready for a new direction once you've spun your web out. They need time to study and become attached to new books for the next web. See page 121 for a list of sources for recommended reading that are updated each year.

# Looking Ahead

Once your classroom library is in good shape, you will have all the keys to weave strong book webs and make your curriculum truly emergent. Let's review:

- High-quality literature invites exploration and contains lessons across the curriculum.

- Tying activities to books helps children make connections, build on previous knowledge, and spend more time with their favorite subjects and characters.

- Open-ended activities make curriculum developmentally appropriate and responsive to the children in your class.

- Inviting parents and other staff to help you weave book webs encourages strong home–school connections and creates lifelong readers.

So what are you waiting for? Go gather a few children, curl up with a great book . . . and see what emerges!

# Getting Started: Sources for Book Reviews and Recommendations

Don't know where to begin? Several organizations compile annual lists of recommended titles. Using these to shop will help you focus your book searches and build a rich classroom library that includes the latest gems.

## The Boston Globe-Horn Book Awards

Lists of past winners can be found at www.hbook.com/bghb2004 .shtml.

## The Randolph Caldecott Medal

This award for best picture-book art is presented by the American Library Association. Winning titles are widely available and tend to stay in print. Past winners and criteria can be found on its Web site: www.ala.org.

## The Chicago Public Library's Best of the Best

Available online at www.chipublib.org/008subject/003cya/ bestofbest/best04_intro.html.

## CLRC Reference Service

The University of Minnesota's Children's Literature Research Collections staff will answer reference questions about children's literature. E-mail clrc@umn.edu with your question. Queries are limited to fifteen minutes of research time. Online: http://special .lib.umn.edu/clrc/researchtools.php.

## The Children's Literature Network

A nonprofit organization serving the upper Midwest, CLN provides encouragement, education, and programming (including book lists and activity ideas) for "adults who are passionate about encouraging kids to read," as its Web site states. Online: www.childrensliteraturenetwork.org.

## The Coretta Scott King Award

This award is sponsored by the American Library Association "to commemorate and foster the life, works and dreams" of Dr. Martin Luther King Jr. and to honor his wife, Coretta Scott King, "for her courage and determination to continue the work for peace and world brotherhood." Online: www.ala.org.

## The Parents' Choice Foundation Book Awards

The Parents' Choice Foundation is the nation's oldest not-for-profit evaluator of children's educational products. Archived award lists are available online: www.parentschoice.org/get _direct.cfm?cat=p_boo.

## The Charlotte Zolotow Award

Sponsored by the Cooperative Children's Book Center, University of Wisconsin–Madison, this award is given to the author of the best picture-book text published in the United States in the preceding year. Online: www.soemadison.wisc.edu/ccbc/books/ zolotow.asp.

# References

Brown, Margaret Wise. 1947. *Goodnight moon.* New York: Harper.

Jones, Guy W., and Sally Moomaw. 2002. *Lessons from turtle island: Native curriculum in early childhood classrooms.* St. Paul: Redleaf Press.

Martin, Bill, Jr., and John Archambault. 1989. *Chicka chicka boom boom.* New York: Simon and Schuster.

McBratney, Sam. 1995. *Guess how much I love you.* Cambridge, Mass.: Candlewick.

Milne, A. A. 1926. *When we were very young.* New York: Dutton.

Mosel, Arlene. 1968. *Tikki tikki tembo.* New York: Henry Holt.

Page, Robin. 2003. *What do you do with a tail like this?* Boston: Houghton-Mifflin.

Rand, Donna, Toni Trent Parker, and Sheila Foster. 1998. *Black books galore! Guide to great African American children's books.* New York: John Wiley & Sons.

Sendak, Maurice. 1964. *Where the wild things are.* New York: HarperTrophy.

Shannon, David. 1998. *No, David!* New York: Blue Sky.

Shaw, Charles. 1947. *It looked like spill milk.* New York: HarperCollins.

Slapin, Beverly, and Doris Seale. 1998. *Through Indian eyes: The native experience in books for children.* Berkeley, Calif.: Oyatc.

Stevenson, Robert Louis. 1999. *A child's garden of verses.* New York: Simon and Schuster.

Trelease, Jim. 1982. *The read-aloud handbook.* New York: Penguin.

Wolpert, Ellen, and the Committee for Boston Public Housing. 1999. *Start seeing diversity.* St. Paul: Redleaf Press.

Wood, Don and Audrey. 1990. *The little mouse, the red ripe strawberry, and the big hungry bear.* New York: Child's Play International.

Zolotow, Charlotte. 1972. *William's doll.* New York: HarperCollins.

# Other Resources from Redleaf Press

**MORE THAN LETTERS: LITERACY ACTIVITIES FOR PRESCHOOL, KINDERGARTEN, AND FIRST GRADE**

*by Sally Moomaw and Brenda Hieronymus*

*More Than Letters* contains dozens of fun and engaging ideas for creating a literacy-rich classroom.

**USE YOUR WORDS: HOW TEACHER TALK HELPS CHILDREN LEARN**

*by Carol Garhart Mooney*

Designed to help teaching adults think about what they say to children, as well as how they say it, *Use Your Words* examines the connection between the ways teachers speak and the ways children behave and learn.

**SIGN TO LEARN: AMERICAN SIGN LANGUAGE IN THE EARLY CHILDHOOD CLASSROOM**

*by Kirsten Dennis and Tressa Azpiri*

*Sign to Learn* is the first complete introduction to appropriate sign language curriculum for hearing preschoolers. In this unique resource, teachers will learn how to integrate American Sign Language (ASL) into their classroom to enhance the academic, social, and emotional development of children, as well as to respectfully introduce them to Deaf culture.

**THEME KITS MADE EASY**

*by Leslie Silk Eslinger*

*Theme Kits Made Easy* contains a tested method for putting together creative kits using dozens of theme suggestions. Create your own kits using theme ideas like Farm, Naptime, and Three Billy Goats Gruff. Includes suggestions for choosing anti-bias materials and resources.

**REFLECTING CHILDREN'S LIVES: A HANDBOOK FOR PLANNING CHILD-CENTERED CURRICULUM**

*by Deb Curtis and Margie Carter*

Keep children and childhood at the center of your curriculum and rethink ideas about scheduling, observation, play, materials, space, and emergent themes with these original approaches.

**FOCUSED EARLY LEARNING: A PLANNING FRAMEWORK FOR TEACHING YOUNG CHILDREN**

*by Gaye Gronlund*

*Focused Early Learning* provides a simple and innovative framework for organizing teaching plans into a realistic, classroom-based format that focuses on the unique needs of each child.

**800-423-8309**
**www.redleafpress.org**